SUCCESSFUL BUSINESS PROCESS MANAGEMENT

SUCCESSFUL BUSINESS PROCESS MANAGEMENT

What You Need to Know to Get Results

PAULA K. BERMAN

AMACOM

AMERICAN MANAGEMENT ASSOCIATION

New York • Atlanta • Brussels • Chicago • Mexico City • San Francisco
Shanghai • Tokyo • Toronto • Washington, D.C.

This publication is designed to provide accurate and authoritative information in regard to the subject matter covered. It is sold with the understanding that the publisher is not engaged in rendering legal, accounting, or other professional service. If legal advice or other expert assistance is required, the services of a competent professional person should be sought.

Library of Congress Cataloging-in-Publication Data
Berman, Paula K.
  Successful business process management : what you need to know to get results / Paula K. Berman.
    pages cm
  Includes index.
  ISBN-13: 978-0-8144-3401-7 (hardcover)
  ISBN-10: 0-8144-3401-0 (hardcover)
  1. Workflow—Management. 2. Organizational effectiveness—Management. 3. Industrial management. I. Title.
  HD62.17.B47 2014
  658—dc23   2013041830

About AMA
American Management Association (www.amanet.org) is a world leader in talent development, advancing the skills of individuals to drive business success. Our mission is to support the goals of individuals and organizations through a complete range of products and services, including classroom and virtual seminars, webcasts, webinars, podcasts, conferences, corporate and government solutions, business books, and research. AMA's approach to improving performance combines experiential learning—learning through doing—with opportunities for ongoing professional growth at every step of one's career journey.

Printing number
10 9 8 7 6 5 4 3 2 1

CONTENTS

PART THREE   CREATING OR REVISING
                A PROCEDURE

PART FOUR   MAKING PROCEDURES REAL

SUCCESSFUL
BUSINESS
PROCESS
MANAGEMENT

INTRODUCTION

BEFORE WE PLUNGE INTO the details of business process management, it will be useful to begin with a description of what *Successful Business Process Management* is, why I wrote it, who it is written for, and how it is structured, because for this book to be helpful, it has to be a discussion. You need to bring your own opinions and experiences, together with an understanding of your business and company culture. In order to make processes and procedures work for your company, you need to tailor them to fit, because there is no magic bullet and no one-size-fits-all approach.

There are tools and methods that are applicable in many cases, but you'll need to use your own judgment: You *can* drive a nail with the end of a screwdriver, but it's not an efficient way to work and someone is likely to get hurt along the way. A similar thing can happen if you try to use the wrong tools to create process solutions that don't fit your problems. For this reason, I'm going to avoid jargon and management-speak in favor of plain language and simple ideas that can be adapted to provide the value you need.

WHAT THIS BOOK IS

In the chapters that follow, I discuss the basic principles of good processes, starting with fundamental ideas. I explain how a process system works (and how to create and maintain one), how to document standard processes so you have something your process users can read and follow, and how to put that documented process in place as a standard way of working that will remain effective over time. I also provide methods that will enable you to use your own work experience to understand your company's needs, create processes that meet them, and ensure that those processes are optimized, in place, and working correctly in order to achieve your organization's goals. Whether you are a member of a quality department, a manager, a project leader, or the person who will be performing your process as part of your normal work, you can make your processes effective and productive.

This book might seem simple and almost naive compared to some books and articles on this topic. I am not pitching tools that can automate everything for you, I am not instructing you on the latest object modeling methodology, and I am not promising you a silver bullet cure for everything that ails your company. This is not intended as a criticism; there are lots of good tools and methodologies out there, some of which can make your life and your process management much easier—but you need to understand the basics in order to choose the right ones.

No matter what methods you use, you have to consider the needs of your company and engage your own common sense in deciding how to model your business, in figuring out what procedures you need, and in determining what to include in those procedures. Having standardized procedures will not automatically increase your revenue, decrease your time to market, improve your flexibility, or enhance your creativity—but having a good process system, choosing the right procedures, and keeping them flexible can do all those things. Modeling tools and process improvement methods can facilitate your work and provide visibility into your processes' interactions and performance. What they can't do is substitute for understanding what you're doing at a fundamental level.

WHO THIS BOOK IS FOR

Successful Business Process Management is written for individuals who need to create, implement, control, manage, or understand business processes or process systems. Most of all, it's written for people in the trenches, the ones who own or need to create a process or a system of processes. It can also be used to help higher-level managers understand the need for and function of processes and process systems, as well as how to manage those systems.

Typically, process work falls either to people in a process improvement or quality role, or to those who actually perform the process (or their manager). Each of these groups is prone to its own set of issues. Whatever your background or current position, this book can help you understand business process management in order to create and implement processes that work for your company without falling into one of several common pitfalls.

Business analysts and others in designated process-centric roles sometimes operate with an ivory tower mentality, in that they tend to focus on discussions with each other, convincing top management that "Important Work" is going on and satisfying auditors. This risk is especially high when they are cloistered in a separate department or when work is structured so that they interact with each other more than with people in the line organization. If this sounds like an issue you face, this book can provide guidance to help you make sure that your processes and systems serve your business and your internal customers by providing real value.

Conversely, individuals actually involved in performing processes may not understand why they need to take time away from "real work" in order to merely write about work. Too often they do this grudgingly, writing the document in the required format and then forgetting about it. If you are one of these people, I hope to provide an explanation of how good processes can help improve the quality of your work, along with streamlined methods to create lightweight and flexible processes to improve the quality of your outputs without adding administrative waste.

Managers in charge of the creation and implementation of processes that are used by large and diverse groups of employees or by more than one department must guide groups of people with differing attitudes and skills into developing and operating processes that work smoothly together. This can be a real challenge, especially if some or most of those people are not used to thinking about their work from a process point of view.

One of my goals in writing this book is to help you be sure that you spend your efforts only on work that counts: work that makes you and your coworkers more productive, improves your business, and provides transparency to management. In my experience, people who write processes most often learn how to do so on the job, and they may or may not have training on how to do it. Most of the experts who create process systems have been educated in engineering or business or a related field and have become experts in process work through on-the-job experience. I want to assist you in advancing along the path to becoming one of those experts. In this book, I explain what to do, why to do it, and how to combine the general concepts of process management with what you've already learned from your own experience.

What you need are processes tailored to your business: your industry, your company size, your company culture, and your applicable standards. No universal solution fits all companies. To end up with the right system for your business, you need to engage with the ideas I present. Argue back! Use your own experience, benchmarking data, or other references to figure out what processes your company needs. Think about what works and what doesn't for your people. Consider how best to help them accept and foster change. Take my ideas and run with them: Discuss them with your peers and stakeholders (you don't have to say which parts are from me), pay attention to your own experiences, and become the expert on your processes.

Throughout this book, I assume that you are in a position of leadership in process initiatives in your company, whether you are taking that initiative on your own or have been assigned to improve your processes and process system. I also assume that you have some time to devote to this and backing from at least someone in management to try to implement process improvement, though you also may need to convince others. Finally, I assume that you have a thorough knowledge of your company, business climate, and company culture so that you can make good decisions about customizing your processes to your own business—which I believe is crucial to their success.

WHY I WROTE THIS BOOK

To be completely honest, I mostly wrote this book out of frustration. Isn't that why anyone writes a book—because the one they want to read doesn't already exist?

Few books have been published on the topic of business processes and process management compared to the huge number of books on project management, yet the two topics often go hand in hand—a large percentage of business projects are designed to create more efficient ways of working, a.k.a. good standard processes. There are some good books on the topic of business processes and process management out there, but you have to look for them. You can't just walk into an average bookstore and find them on the shelf (as I learned when doing research for this book). I see a need for a book that is reasonably short and very concrete, explains the basics of business processes, and covers corporate processes from a company-wide systemic viewpoint, helping you to figure out what you need to do and why, in ways you can make clear to your own management.

Much of my own knowledge about good processes was acquired on the job, which is a slow way to learn, but a thorough one. My first exposure to process systems was as a young engineer working on flight simulators and helicopters at companies like Raytheon and Boeing. At the time, because no one ever explained the systems and the reasons behind them, I felt like I was drowning in unnecessary red tape. Later in my career, as a quality manager at companies like Honeywell Aerospace and ASML (a leader in semiconductor equipment), I tried to avoid giving others that red-tape feeling by creating processes, process models, and quality systems that made sense to the people who use them. I've worked with companies that had too few processes, where everything was done ad hoc so that much work was performed inefficiently, as well as companies with too much process, forcing people to do unneeded work. In this book, just as in a good process, I hope to pass on what I've learned from those experiences.

In particular, I've come to believe that as a company grows, there's a moment where standardized, documented processes become necessary. It's better to get there ahead of the need, just as a growing city needs to build highways before the roads are totally jammed. When a company is starting up, everyone knows everyone else and works together closely. Everyone is an expert, or at least the most expert person on hand. Everyone is figuring out how to do things for the first time. Later on, as the company grows, a day arrives when there are lots of employees, most of whom haven't been there from the beginning. They don't know the ways that have evolved for doing things, or the reasons for them, and they may be creating their own ways of working. Because the company is now too big for everyone to know exactly what everyone else is working on, people are either retreading ground that has already been walked or creating incompatibilities with each other. It's very often true that there's no one right way of working, but that it would be useful if everyone worked in the same way, even if it's only one of many possible ways to do things.

I believe as well in the value of incremental improvement. A lot of process improvement fads have come and gone, with the claim made that you can gain value only by totally reengineering your processes from the ground up. If you get the chance or can achieve the backing to create an entire process system from scratch, that's great—but more often you start with an existing system and don't have the time or the other resources to change everything at once. Even if you need to work in one process area at a time, I believe you can make material gains in your company's efficiency, effectiveness, and general pleasantness as a place to work—and each success gains you more experience and credibility for the next project.

KEY MESSAGES

Here's where I spoil the suspense at the beginning! Many ideas and useful tips are presented throughout this book, but the main points can be boiled down to three simple, central concepts:

1. Processes work best when they are part of a managed and coherent system. Otherwise, at best you have built an island of sanity in a sea of chaos.

2. Once you've defined and documented a procedure, you're not done with it. To make it useful, you need to launch it successfully and then monitor, measure, and improve it on an ongoing basis.

3. There is no single right way to build a process or process system. Some good ones are simple and some good ones are elaborate, and there are many ways to structure them. To have one that works for your business, you need to customize it.

HOW THIS BOOK IS STRUCTURED

This book has five parts. Part 1 provides necessary information about processes and procedures. Part 2 addresses topics you need to understand to ensure that the structure and environment necessary for your processes are present, enabling the effective creation and management of your process system. Parts 3 and 4 help you to create or revise standard documented processes, and enable you to roll out new or changed processes and make sure they're in place, being followed, and having the intended effect. Part 5 is devoted to developing skills that you'll find useful along the way.

One unfortunate side effect of this structure is that it makes it look like you do everything in order, one step at a time: Put a process system in place and perfect it, document a process, and only then figure out how to launch it and manage its operation. That's a pleasant fiction, but it's neither true nor effective in the real world. The steps overlap and feed back to each other; for example, you may already have standard documented processes in place but feel the need to develop a new system to organize and visualize your processes and their interfaces. When creating a new process, you should develop a plan for rolling it out before you've finished the documentation, and at the same time figure out what process data you will monitor. It's not a good idea to wait until everything is documented and perfect before you create rollout and control plans. This is inefficient because it forces the rollout to wait until long after the process itself is complete, and because what you learn while planning the rollout may well force changes in the process document. In addition, when monitoring a process to make sure it's working well, you can collect feedback for the next revision of the process.

THE IMPORTANCE OF
KEEPING PROCESSES USABLE

I've seen two trends in the process world that I think are related. One is toward increasing complexity in process diagrams, documented processes, and process systems, to the point where average employees can't understand them without training, even if they already understand the relevant business area and way of working. The other trend is for processes to be only partially completed: either documented but never truly deployed and operational, or implicitly agreed upon but never written down to make sure everyone understands them in the same way. This second development is really less of a trend than an ongoing problem that's always existed. I think, though, that the trend toward complexity makes this development worse: People are not likely to make great efforts to use a process or system they don't understand. With *Successful Business Process Management*, I hope to help you choose and document the processes that are right for your company and then embed them in your organization as an effective way to work.

PART ONE

Reviewing the Definitions

CHAPTER 1

Understanding Processes and Procedures

LET'S START FROM THE VERY BEGINNING, with definitions of some essential terms. This is an important thing to do any time you're working on process documentation. Words are all you have to convey your ideas, but in many cases people understand the same words in different ways. That's especially true for seemingly simple terms like "process." You don't want to learn, several days or weeks into a project, that the conversations you thought you were having sounded very different to the other people involved. Thus, clear definitions are critical to getting everyone on the same page.

Once we have a shared understanding of processes and related topics, we can go on to consider why they're important. Obviously, I think processes matter, as a way of conducting business effectively. You probably do too, since you're reading this book, but we need to be specific about *how* they matter and what aspects of them are important in order to ensure that our processes realize the goals we have for them.

WHAT ARE PROCESSES AND PROCEDURES?

The terms "process" and "procedure" get used a lot, sometimes interchangeably, and sometimes to mean very different things. "Work instruction" is another phrase that can carry subtly different meanings. For this reason, I'm providing my definition of these terms below. When you read any book or article on the topic of process improvement, it's important to check the definitions to make sure you understand what the author means.

What Is a Process?

A *process* is a set of interrelated activities designed to transform inputs into outputs. It gets you from where you are to where you want to be. An effective process realizes planned activities and achieves planned results. If you've been working with processes, you probably already understand this concept, but we need to agree on definitions for the terms involved in the process in order to be able to discuss and analyze it.

- An *input* is what you already have or expect to receive in time to start a step/activity. An input may be intangible, such as time, a customer's need, or an engineer's expertise, or it may be a physical object, such as a raw material or part. It may include something that will be changed in some way during the course of the process, such as a component that will be assembled into a final product, or it can include a resource that will not be changed, such as money or a piece of factory equipment.

- An *output* is what you want to deliver to the customer so the next step/activity can proceed. (The customer of a process may be internal—within your company—or external—the end customer who is paying for your product or service.) In the process of selling an ebook to a customer, the input is the book file and the customer's computer or e-reader plus money and an Internet or mobile-phone delivery system, and the output is the book file that resides on a device from which the customer can read it. As you can see in this example, not all outputs are tangible or physical objects. However, outputs do need to be measurable. An output of a customer relationship process could be customer satisfaction, but that needs to be measured by customer surveys or other methods.

- A *trigger* is the signal for a process to start. It may be time-based (a yearly audit), condition-based (a restock for a vending machine whenever it indicates that it is low on supplies), or based on the completion of another process (an installation of wheels on a toy car after the chassis is painted).

- A process always has a *customer*, but the customer (as stated above) may be either external or internal. The simplest way to say it is that the customer is whoever needs the output of the process.

For example, the process by which an engineer designs a component is triggered by the need for a new component. (The old one may be faulty, or a new product design may require entirely new components.) The inputs include customer requirements and data of raw materials, plus any applicable standards, design tooling, time, and expertise. The output is a finished and documented design. The customers are other engineers and techs who will use the design to build the new product. During the process, the engineer converts the customer requirements (which could be in a customer's head or could come from market analysis) into measurable technical requirements, creates a design, verifies that it meets those requirements, and then validates the design by building and testing a prototype. Those activities make up a process.

What Is a Procedure?

A *procedure* is a way of carrying out a process or activity. It outlines who performs the process activities and in what order and provides other relevant information (though a higher-level procedure does not provide step-by-step instructions to perform each task). In this book, I always use the term "procedure" to refer to a *standardized, documented* set of ordered activities, and the term "process" to refer to the set of activities documented in a procedure.

A procedure document generally consists of a *process map*—a graphical representation of the steps in a process and how they fit together—plus supporting explanation and other needed text. Process maps can be nested: that is, one box in a higher-level process map can be developed into a whole lower-level process map of its own. The rest of a procedure document explains its scope and goals and provides more information about each step in the process map and who performs it, as well as any other necessary information, such as roles and responsibilities, records, or references to related documents.

The lowest-level procedures, often called *work instructions*, define specifically how to perform a task in detail, step-by-step. Work instructions are always documented and are generally carried out by one person or a small team. Unlike other procedures, very linear work instructions may not need process maps.

WHAT IS A PROCESS SYSTEM?

A *process system* is a model of the business, showing how processes fit together to meet the goals of the company. It provides a structure in which work instructions fit into processes, and processes fit together to describe the working of the business as a whole. A process system is a powerful tool for understanding the working of the business and improving it, by spotting gaps where work isn't getting done correctly or identifying inefficiencies where more resources are used than are needed.

Processes are interconnected because the output from one process becomes the input for another process. In effect, processes are "glued" together by means of such input-output relationships. It is not unusual to learn that one department values and depends on inputs that another department does not take seriously and has no standard processes to produce. Creating the process system can provide the impetus for important and necessary conversations between different groups.

A process system generally has some kind of overview of the system at the top level, with a hierarchy of increasingly detailed procedures below that. This top-level overview may be contained in a *Quality*

Manual, the document defining a company's quality policy and quality system. Typically, the Quality Manual contains a statement of the company's commitment to quality, top management's responsibilities, an overview of the process system and other systems for ensuring quality in the company's products or services, and an explanation of how relevant quality standards are met.

WHAT ARE PROCEDURES FOR?
(OR WHY SHOULD YOU BOTHER?)

In many companies, if you ask average employees what their standard procedures are for, you might be get answers like: "To keep the quality people happy," "To get in the way of real work," "I don't know but management wants them," or even "So we can be certified to the ISO 9001 standard."

This is bad.

Having procedures for the sake of being able to say you have them is waste. ("Waste" is defined as spending time or other resources on activities that do not contribute directly to the product, including service products, or not doing something correctly the first time.) If an activity can be removed without detriment to the company's long-term goals—including quality products/services, satisfied customers, and thriving employees—it is waste. Unused procedures run through paper, digital storage space, and, most of all, time. As Benjamin Franklin said, "Do not squander time, for that is the stuff life is made of." It's also the stuff a business is made of. If you're wasting time creating unused procedures, you're not doing something more useful.

Well-chosen standard business processes, captured into documented procedures and deployed effectively, provide real value to the organization in lots of different ways:

- *They provide a model of the business. A*t the highest level, a process system provides a model of how an entire business operates. This model and the processes that constitute it ensure that everyone in the company is working from the same basic assumptions of how the company functions.

- *They offer a concrete path to follow to meet the business's core mission.* Many businesses say that they want to satisfy the customer's needs with world-class products or services, or words to that effect. The right procedures can supply the concrete steps to follow to ensure that daily operations are carried out in a way that is consistent with your goals.

- *They ensure that interfaces are agreed upon.* Procedures serve as interface agreements between company divisions, departments, teams, and individuals. Defining the inputs and outputs of each process, and mapping how the processes fit together, allows you to find gaps, identify waste, and create more efficient ways of operation.

- *They multiply expertise, helping new employees to become productive faster.* A detailed work instruction created by an expert to clearly document how he performs a standard task can then be followed by someone with less knowledge and experience. The procedure can also tell newer or less experienced employees where to find the other information they need to do their work. This is especially critical in cases where you are expanding rapidly and bringing in many new people or when you have high employee turnover. It also means that your experts can simply refer people to the appropriate procedure, instead of having to answer every question themselves.

- *They standardize ways of working.* Making sure everyone who performs this process has the same understanding of it and performs it in the same way is critical. It's often true that there's more than one right way to do it—but since there are always even more ways to do it *wrong*, it's valuable to choose one of those right ways (the best one, if there is such a thing) and make sure everyone follows it. This single way of working reduces variation in the outputs of the process, making them more consistent, which then helps to further processes down the line.

- *They allow improvements.* There's a saying that "You can't improve what you don't measure." It's not entirely true, but if you don't thoroughly understand your process, you'll never know if you actually did improve it, or by how much. "Measure" in this case means not only taking metrics but also understanding what the current process is—not just what it's supposed to be, but what it really is. The basic steps of process improvement are to determine what your goals for the process are, study the existing situation, analyze where it falls short, and then make improvements and measure them.

- *They avoid single points of failure.* If important company processes that are not standardized and documented are carried out by only one person (or just a few people), and then if that expert leaves the company or is out sick, the process has to be reinvented by others. Meanwhile, paychecks or orders can be delayed, or errors can be made that take months to correct or even find. (This sounds extreme, but it's based on a real-life example.)

- *They offer assurance of quality to your customers.* As customers grow more demanding in business areas where quality is critical, they may ask to be shown your process system in order to be assured of your quality of production and service.

- *They pass certification audits.* This includes audits for certification of compliance with industry standards, such as ISO 9001, ISO 14001, AS9100, and SAE. Note that this item is listed *last*. I believe that passing audits and gaining certification are properly a byproduct of a good working process system, not the main goal. However, ISO 9001 and other such standards are actually good and reasonable documents. If you're starting to build a process system from scratch, they can offer useful guidance to what you need.

WHEN IS A PROCESS OR PROCEDURE NEEDED?

Actually, a process is always needed because it consists of the activities you do that get you from "work undone" to "work done." What you don't always need is a standardized, documented process—a procedure. You need a procedure:

- When you have multiple people or groups of people whom you want to perform an activity in the same way. This especially applies when some of those people have less training and expertise than others, and you want them to be able to perform to the same specifications.

- When you need to train new employees in how to perform a standard task.

- When a process is complex and its output is critical, either because it's delivered to an external customer or because it's the input to another process.

- When the procedure is required by your standards or by your own business model.

- When you need the ability to have a business-critical process performed by people who don't usually do it, in case of illness, vacation, or an emergency.

- When people who are not performing the work (e.g., managers) need to understand the process.

- When you need to improve a process in a measurable way.

WHEN IS A PROCEDURE NOT NEEDED?

You don't need a documented procedure for simple actions that are performed by a single experienced individual, though it may still be useful to have validation tests or templates for some outputs. You also don't always need a procedure to produce some outputs that are used only internally by a small organization, though in many cases it may be useful to have one.

You don't need a complete procedure when a simple checklist will do. You don't need low-level, detailed instructions for every action, either. Document your procedures to the level of detail that is useful, and no further.

Use the following checklist to determine when a procedure is needed:

❑ Will anyone ever look at the procedure again?

❑ Will it be used for training?

❑ Do you often have new people who need to be trained?

❑ Is the process so critical to the business that it must be done perfectly?

❑ Would it reduce waste of time or resources to have the process documented?

❑ Would it help save time for your experts by reducing the number of questions that people ask them?

❑ Is it required by any standard or certification?

❑ Does the process involve more than one organization, or is it used by people in different geographic regions?

❑ Do you need to improve or optimize the process?

If the answer to all of these is "no," then you don't need a documented procedure.

There are solid reasons for not having more procedures than you need. Obviously, it wastes time and effort to create and implement them, and unnecessary documentation also clogs up your process system. Unless your system is extremely well organized and intuitive, having more documentation than you need makes it more difficult for people to find the processes they *do* need. A more subtle point is that when employees see a lot of procedures that are not useful, it is harder for them to trust that most of the processes in the system do have value. This tends to decrease their respect for the whole system, which can make them less likely to follow and use the procedures that matter or to create new ones when needed.

Unused procedures are an audit trap as well. Auditors look for documented procedures and then go on to determine whether they are followed and whether appropriate records are kept. If procedures don't specify what records should be kept to verify their execution, that omission is reported as a weakness in the procedure. If procedures indicate that records should be kept and the (lack of) records show they were not followed, that can lead to an audit finding, and in extreme cases to the loss of customer confidence or of certification to a standard.

The issues listed in the checklist above all come down to two important questions: (1) Will a procedure make it easier for you to meet your customers' needs? (2) Will it help you do a better job meeting your customers' needs? It's OK if a "yes" answer to these questions is indirect (such as "Yes, because our Employee Evaluation Procedure helps us keep and reward the best people" or "Yes, because our Document Control Procedure enables the rest of the procedures required to support our business and produce our product"). A "no" answer is a sign that you should consider whether you can do without that procedure.

WHEN DO YOU NEED TO ADD, IMPROVE, OR RESTRUCTURE PROCESSES?

In much of this book I talk about creating new procedures or process systems. However, the likelihood is that you already have many standard processes, some or many documented procedures, and possibly a process system in place. You probably need to add or revamp one or more processes if you're seeing some of the following issues:

- Productivity not meeting reasonable targets

- Frequent misunderstandings in your company about who needs to deliver what to whom

- Difficulty embedding measurable and reliable improvements

- New people taking too long to come up to speed and reach expected levels of productivity

- A shared sense that people in your company are wasting (or worse, being forced to waste) large amounts of time and energy as they try to get their work done, or that the process could be significantly more efficient than it is

- Complaints from customers that your company is not sufficiently responsive to their issues

- Inconsistent results in output quality, time to complete process, resources needed, or other key factors

If you need to improve your existing processes, you can use the same methods to revise a procedure as to document a new one. You will need to roll out and manage changes in the same way—change is change, whether it's putting something new in place or adapting something old.

Avoiding Unnecessary Complexity

As you move on to create or revise process systems and standardized processes, bear these two rules in mind. They'll help you create a useful system rather than a red-tape obstacle:

Rule S: Keep procedures as *simple* as possible but not simpler. Include only the level of detail that is actually useful for the reader of each specific case.

Rule M: Keep the number and length of procedures to a *minimum* by creating only the procedures that provide value. Similarly, avoid adding unnecessary information inside procedures.

PART TWO

Building an Effective Process System

CHAPTER 2

Creating the Structure of Your Process System

I'VE COME TO BELIEVE, through experience, that having a bunch of unorganized processes is just not enough. It might be better than trying to figure out each task from scratch every time, but it's not the most efficient way to run a business. For that, you need to organize your processes into a process system. Just as having a standard process allows you to perform a series of tasks in a repeatable way—seeing where improvements need to be made and then whether those improvements worked as expected—a well-organized process system takes the same idea to the next level. With such a system, you can not only execute each process efficiently but also see how the processes fit together. Without a process system, you may not be able to tell when you have the right processes in place. The consequences of this might be that you don't have the needed inputs ready for one process because another isn't in place to produce them; that you waste time and effort by executing a process that isn't actually needed; or that you don't have an efficient way to create new processes, publish them, or put them in place and monitor their operation.

You are a logical and experienced person, so now you're probably asking, "If process systems are so important, how has my company been doing without one this long?" The answer is that it hasn't. In fact, your company probably has several systems, all undocumented and un-planned. The question is whether those systems are as effective as they could be. Humans tend to evolve systems around themselves even when they aren't trying to; you develop your normal ways of working, con-sciously or not, and they don't exist in a vacuum.

The danger is that systems that just naturally grow up without any attention being paid to their development tend to be inefficient, in-complete, and not understood in the same way by all users. Different groups of workers may each have their own system, so that existing processes may not align well across groups. No one is consciously checking to see whether any processes are missing, until people are di-rectly hurt by the lack of one that's needed, and no one may notice if unneeded work is being done because two groups have overlapping processes. Any employee who creates procedures naturally tends to build and launch them in the same way each time, but different em-ployees do it in different ways, which may or may not work for the process users. A single, comprehensive, and well-organized process sys-tem can prevent these consequences.

In an ideal world, a good process system would be in place before any processes are created. However, I've never gotten to work from a completely clean slate, and you probably won't either. You probably already have a corporate mission, values, and goals, whether stated or implicit, but chances are that your existing processes weren't particularly designed with those in mind. Those processes may be formal proce-dures, a flowchart on a webpage, or just several mutually agreed-upon ways of working that somehow need to be linked together into a co-herent system. That's OK—not ideal, but definitely OK.

The chapters in Part 2 explain how to create a new process system from the ground up, but if you do have an existing documented system, don't start from scratch unless there's good reason for doing it that way.

Read this chapter and think about how you can improve your existing system in less invasive ways, or whether there's a real need to create a new one. (See also the final section of Chapter 4, "Knowing When a Process System Requires Improvement.")

BEGINNING TO CREATE A PROCESS SYSTEM

A process system is a map of how a company works. An effective one is a shared big picture that allows you and your colleagues to see how your processes fit together and where they don't. This provides a basis to manage improvements, keeping them coordinated and compatible.

A process system includes a structure and a set of standard rules that govern your company's processes. It defines the hierarchical relationship of your processes, including interfaces among processes on the same level and how they relate to those above and below them in the hierarchy. It controls how your procedures are to be documented and operated, what approvals are needed, and how documents and records are maintained, providing your procedures with a consistent look and feel that allows process users to understand them more quickly because they know how the information in a procedure is organized. An effective process system also includes a coherent system of *version control*, which tracks change history, allows only one person to edit a procedure at a time, and ensures that users always see the latest version of a procedure.

A process system provides a map that you and your colleagues can use to have a shared version of the big picture and to manage improvements, keeping them coordinated and compatible.

DO YOU NEED A STRONG PROCESS SYSTEM
BEFORE CREATING YOUR PROCEDURES?

In an ideal world, yes, you would want a strong process system before creating any processes. You begin to create a process system founded on your basic principles by stating your company's mission, values,

FIGURE 2-1   Linkage Between Levels in a Process Structure

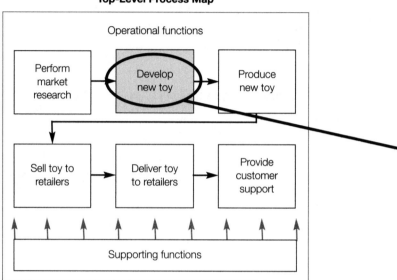

Top-Level Process Map

goals, and policies, including a *quality policy*—a statement of your company's dedication to providing a high-quality product or service. (If you do an online search for "quality policy," you can find many real-life examples.) You then set up a structure and carefully determine what procedures are needed to move you toward your goals in a way that accords with your corporate values and policies. You also create a Quality Manual, a document that explains how you achieve the level of quality you've committed to and provides a brief overview of your process system. From there, you link to a top-level model of your business, and from that you link down through increasingly detailed levels of procedures to your lowest-level work instructions that provide step-by-step guides to daily tasks, as shown in Figure 2-1.

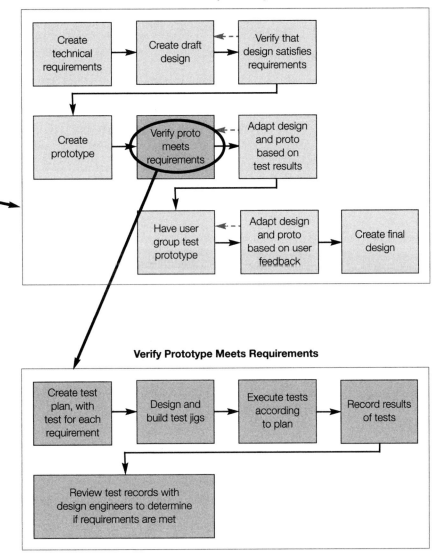

Develop New Toy

Creating a process structure is an iterative process: Even once you have the basic structure developed and agreed to by management and other stakeholders, you need to return to it more than once as you look for gaps (missing processes), mismatched interfaces (when one process' input requirements are not met by another), overlapping processes (where one or more process steps are shown in multiple procedures), and other issues while you work on optimizing the system. One advantage to having a process structure—a hierarchy—is that as you find the gaps, you don't immediately have to fill them. You can plan your work in order of priority. Once you've identified the gaps, you can analyze the current situation to figure out which process issues are most critical, and you can assign placeholders to processes that can be worked out later. Try to build your process system (or revise an existing one) from the top down; if you build bottom up, you're likely to create confusion when you find you need an extra level somewhere, and you won't have a clear view of where gaps exist.

In the real world, you may not be able to start with a blank slate. You might have a partial system in place or some procedures you need to maintain. If you already have some existing procedures or other components of a process system, pay attention to how they fit in and fit together. As you work through developing your process structure, you start getting feedback from your processes to your system and vice versa. You might see gaps where you need a process or procedure and don't have one. For example, perhaps you have a process that you know is crucial to your business, but you realize you have no standard way to guarantee that inputs to that process are of the needed quality. In that case, you'd need a new process to generate those inputs or to ensure that your suppliers do. Or you might have a common process that's always been transmitted by word of mouth (sometimes called "tribal knowledge") but that was never documented in a procedure. If so, you run the risk that information may be transmitted inaccurately or that people might forget steps of the process or do them wrong. You may also find redundancies where two or more procedures contain some of the same tasks. As you develop your hierarchy, look for ways to improve your existing procedures, including adding new ones where they're needed and weeding out old ones that are unnecessary.

DEVELOPING A PROCESS HIERARCHY

When beginning to create a process system—once your mission, vision, and quality policy are known—you can develop a process hierarchy. Start from the top down, beginning with an overview of your business. Usually a business process system contains several levels of process; within the hierarchy I will talk about high-level and low-level processes. A *high-level process* is more abstract and has a broader area of focus than a process at a lower level; it contains less detail but covers a wider range of tasks. A *low-level process* is more detailed and more concrete. Most companies have three or more levels in their process system. The very top level always shows what is to be done, while the lowest level gives detailed instructions for how to perform each task. It's up to the creators of a process system to decide how rigidly to define each intermediate level and whether it is important to keep a similar level of detail in procedures on the same level, or whether it doesn't matter.

An unrealistically simple system for a whole company might look like Figure 2-2, which is a representation of the entire process hierarchy for the hypothetical Imaginary Toy Company. This illustration shows graphically why we don't usually look at an entire process system hierarchy at once. (Don't bother trying to read this figure, which is simply meant to illustrate a structure.) For a large company, there are many more procedures than are shown here. We typically look only at the top level, and then at different segments, such as one top-level process and its next level subprocesses.

At the highest level of the hierarchy is a simple and abstract model of the entire business. For instance, the top-level business model for our hypothetical toy company may contain a process map like the one in Figure 2-3.

You can see that this process map is at a very high level of abstraction. No details are given, and the text in the boxes describes only what is to be done but does not explain how to do it. This figure provides a simple model of a larger and much more complicated reality. Each box in this process map is actually an entire large process of its own that can be shown in a more detailed process map at the next, lower level. For instance, the next level of detail for the "Develop new toy" process might look like Figure 2-4.

FIGURE 2-2 Imaginary Toy Company's Process Overview

FIGURE 2-3 Imaginary Toy Company's Top-Level Process Map

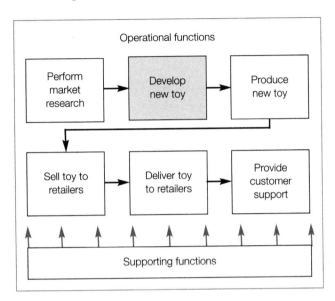

FIGURE 2-4 Imaginary Toy Company's Second-Level
Process Map

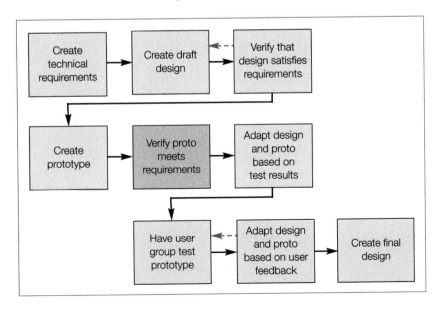

In most cases, so much is going on in each process step that it is useful to break down these tasks even further, into "child" processes. For instance, the process of creating the technical requirements includes studying the market research to determine customer needs, but it also includes consulting applicable laws, industry standards, company rules and guidelines (for instance, about safety, preferred materials, and logos), and principles of usability. The requirements dictated by each of these then need to be stated in concrete and measurable terms, reviewed with team members, and revised as necessary.

One higher-level procedure may be the "parent" of one or more lower-level procedures or work instructions. (A parent/child relationship between procedures means that a task that is just shown as a box on the higher-level procedure is broken down further into a whole process map in the lower-level procedure.) Remember *Rule S* and *Rule M* at every level of your process system; overly complicated procedures (or an abundance of procedures) are only going to annoy people and lead to errors, without contributing any value to your work. Every procedure or work instruction (except the very top one) must have a parent, but not every procedure must have a child. Don't create more levels than you need to make a clear model of your business and to enable employees both to do their own jobs and to understand how they fit into your business.

Defining the Top Level of the Hierarchy

When determining what to include in the top level of your process hierarchy, begin with your corporate vision, mission, and goals, and consider what you need to accomplish them. Take a broad view. Yes, you want to dazzle your customers, but in order to accomplish that efficiently you need employees who have the skills, training, facilities, and support to get their jobs done, and who are not so discontented that they are all looking around for the next job. Speaking generically, most companies do all of the following tasks, which need to be included in their process systems:

- Decide what employees are providing to customers (which includes finding out what customers want by listening to the customers themselves)

- Convince customers they want to buy what the company provides

- Hire the right people

- Provide them with the right training

- Give employees whatever facilities and supplies they need to do their jobs

- Manage the employees

- Design and produce a product, or design a service

- Deliver and ship a product, or perform a service

- Support a product or service

- Ensure that the product or service complies with applicable laws and standards

- Manage their finances

- Manage their customers (perform relationship management, set expectations, respond to complaints, and so forth)

However you design your system, it must include all processes your company needs to perform, and it must be organized in a logical structure. Consider how these processes interrelate and which ones produce outputs that are used by others.

The Quality Manual

The foundation document of your process system should contain or link to your top-level model (such as the one in Figure 2-3). It's common to use a Quality Manual as this document; if you want to be certified to ISO 9001 or similar standards, you are required to have one. If you are not required to have a full Quality Manual, you may still find it useful to have one as the bedrock on which the rest of your *quality system* stands. (In this book, I mostly talk about process systems; a quality system should contain your process system as well as other systems such as audits, product quality assurance, and so forth. Other standards, such as those for environment, health, and safety [EHS], may also require some processes to be part of your process system.) Quality Manuals can vary from a simple restatement of a standard—where every time the standard states "The organization shall ... " the Quality Manual substitutes "This organization does ... "—to an elaborate explanation of all aspects of the quality system.

In general, whichever approach you take, it is best to keep the Quality Manual simple and at a high level of abstraction. Since it governs all of your company's processes, the Quality Manual needs to be kept under very tight control and must be approved by high levels of management. Thus, it is difficult to change. The more details you have, the more often it will need to be changed, or else it becomes incorrect and obsolete. In fact, this is a specific and important case of *Rule S.*

At a minimum, a Quality Manual should contain a statement of your management's commitment to quality, a link to your company's quality policy, a statement that you will adhere to relevant standards (clarifying which ones) and laws (if applicable), and a very broad overview of your organization and quality system. It is a good idea to link your Quality Manual to the top level of your process system instead of incorporating it within the document, so that it does not have to be changed whenever higher-level processes are added, deleted, or altered.

A Top-Level Overview of the Process Structure

The top-level model, like the one in Figure 2-3, may stand alone or may be part of a Quality Manual. All lower-level process maps are typically found within procedures.

If your company is small and not being certified to ISO or similar standards, you may decide not to create a Quality Manual. It is never a good idea to create a document that no one is likely to read. If your company is small enough that everyone interacts closely, and if you're never likely to have a compliance or customer audit, then you may decide that the company's dedication to quality can be read in the daily actions of management and employees, rather than in a formal document. An overview process map may be all you need at the top of your process system.

If you do need to have or choose to have a Quality Manual, you can link to your overview process map from that document. (Use a hyperlink for online documents, or include a description of how to access it in printed documents.) While at other levels a process map is generally part of a more elaborate procedure document, the very top-level process map might not require a documented procedure. Generally, there's so much detail not shown in the box representing each second-level process that it's not sensible or even possible to delineate who performs each task, what records are kept, and so on. Instead, those items are included in the more detailed procedures for each second-level process.

Let's look again at that top-level example from the Imaginary Toy Company in Figure 2-3. Notice that this simple model applies to almost any company that produces a product. You might want to break up the boxes differently (that is, change the scope of the processes), but the basic model is fairly universal. For instance, if the development of new products is central to your company, you might want to list Design > Develop > Test as separate boxes, whereas here I have lumped them together into "Develop new toy." Or if getting parts and components to where they are needed is a major challenge, you may need a separate logistics box, whereas in Figure 2-3 the logistics functions have been lumped into "Produce new toy" and "Deliver toy to retailers."

For a service company, the top-level process map could be similar, as shown in Figure 2-5. Here, I've added a box for "Collect feedback and improve service." There could also be a link back from that box to "Develop new service," since customer feedback might reveal a market niche for a new service offering. Obviously, a similar box could also be added on the product company's top-level process map. In Figure 2-3, I assumed that collecting feedback was part of "Provide customer support" and "Perform market research," and that a toy company was more likely to design a new toy than improve an old one, but you should customize this to whatever is true and appropriate for your business.

The Rest of the Rules

This is probably a good time to introduce another couple of rules:

> *Rule C:* Don't make your system too generic. *Customize* it to your company's business and culture. But bear in mind that *Rule C* must be balanced with another rule:

> *Rule R:* Don't reinvent the wheel. Study common practices in your industry and in similar ones, and *reuse* whatever ideas will work for you.

A feature to notice in both of the process maps in Figures 2–3 and 2–5 is the box along the bottom, "Supporting functions." Often, only operational processes are included in the process system, but supporting processes keep your company functioning, and it can be helpful to think of how everything fits together. All companies have internal support

FIGURE 2-5 Consulting Company's Top-Level Process Map

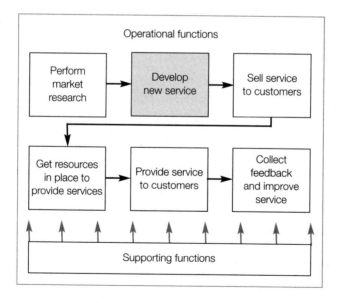

processes (e.g., to make sure everyone gets paid on time), but without taking a systems approach, less critical (but still important) processes may be overlooked. For instance, a coherent process for how to arrange everything new hires need (phone, computer, facilities tour, training, introductions, and so forth) can ensure that they become productive employees in a shorter time.

Use the same thought process that you would for any operational business area to consider whether your company needs standard procedures within HR, IT, finance, legal, facilities, or other supporting groups in your process system. Notice how they relate to each other and to operational processes when deciding how to show them in your top-level process map; you can lump them together, as in Figures 2-3 and 2-5, or separate them into different areas. As with anything else, follow *Rule C* and do what makes the most sense for your business.

Other Ways to Organize Your Top-Level Process Structure

In this book, I often use a process map like the one in Figure 2-3 as an example because it's easy to recognize and understand. However, that isn't the only valid way to organize your processes at the top level. The business model in Figure 2-3 is functional, showing the major activities (processes) of a business. However, in practice, there may be good reasons to do it another way.

My *least* favorite way to organize processes is according to the business's org chart, showing which processes belong to which department. This is problematic for two reasons: (1) It makes it difficult to know how to deal with processes that involve more than one department, and (2) whenever you reorganize your business, you need to revise your top-level process structure. Despite those issues, this may be the easiest structure to get your people to accept, especially if they're new to process thinking or if you have managers who are fiercely protective of their kingdoms. It's better to have a process structure organized by department than not to have a process system at all.

If you are in a highly regulated industry that is held rigidly to a standard, you may find it best to organize your processes along the lines of that standard. Here's an example:

Raj, a quality manager with experience in a variety of industries, takes a job with Sirop Aerospace. Raj has strong opinions about process management and prefers an activity-based approach, but he finds that he has inherited a process structure based on AS9100, the aerospace standard—procedure documents are even numbered according to the standard's table of contents. The company's processes are overly complicated and not well followed, which is why the company hired Raj in the first place.

Raj changes his original plan and decides to focus on improving (and simplifying!) processes instead of changing the overall structure. Because of his company's strong need to comply to the standard, the current process structure is well understood and accepted by management, employees, and customers alike. It is a logical organization that fits the business well, and AS9100, which is very similar to ISO 9001, is a short and sensible standard. Raj feels a bit sorry to stay with this text-based top-level structure instead of the simple graphics he's used to, but by doing so, he dodges the large risks inherent in selling a huge structural change, avoids the extra work of fixing something that wasn't broken, makes it easier to pass audits for compliance to the standard, and uses the knowledge of experts in the industry as embodied in the standard.

Designating the Process Owner

A *process owner* is the person who is accountable for making sure that the procedure is correct and current and that it is followed by process users. The process owner may not be the author of the procedure or the project leader of process improvement initiatives, but the people in those roles act under her authority. As you define procedures at each level, make sure that each one has a designated process owner. This person's role must be agreed upon not only by management but by the owner herself. The process owner may choose to designate someone else, or multiple people, to do the actual work of documenting, rolling out, and maintaining the process, but the process owner has the responsibility to make sure those things get done right.

Obviously, the process owner needs to thoroughly understand and agree with the process goals. She does not need to be the ultimate authority on the mechanics of the process but does need a basic understanding of how it works. She also needs sufficient resources and authority to ensure that the process gets documented and turned into functioning reality. This may mean that process work is budgeted into her workload, or it could mean that she has the authority to designate other people, including content experts, to get the work done. Either way, the success of the project needs to be a part of the goals and targets on which the process owner's performance is judged.

The required hierarchical level of a process owner is not the same for all processes. Processes at a higher level in the hierarchy or those that are more crucial to the business need to be owned by someone senior in the company, while lower-level or less critical processes can be owned by someone closer to the actual task.

A good rule of thumb is to give the ownership role to the lowest-level person in the management hierarchy who has sufficient authority to make the process happen. If ownership is assigned to someone who lacks this authority, the consequences are obvious: The process won't succeed. If ownership is assigned to someone too senior, the results can be just as bad: The process gets overlooked because the senior manager lacks time to be directly involved. To reiterate a crucial point, the process performance needs to be one of the criteria on which the process owner's performance is appraised; therefore, the owner's workload needs to include planned time to manage the process, including creation or revision, if necessary. Much of the work can be delegated, but the process owner must understand and approve the changes.

When you decide who owns a process, consider the future as well as the present. The process owner (or her designate) is involved in changes to the process, approves the final version, and is responsible for the success of the rollout, but she is also in charge of managing the process once it's in place. This includes monitoring process indicators to ensure that the process is working (of course, data can also be assembled by someone else and reported to the process owner) and determining when the process needs further improvement. Improvement may be required when the process is not being followed correctly, when it is being followed but is not having the intended effect, when the business changes, or when there's an opportunity to make it perform better.

Defining High-Level Procedures

Procedures at high levels of the hierarchy describe what actions must be taken or what tasks must be completed to follow a process, but they do not provide instructions for *how* to do them. They are most useful for managers and others who work with the big picture, as well as to explain the company's workings to new hires. They do the following: show how tasks link together; help you establish where you have gaps (when someone or some department is not getting what's needed to work effectively or efficiently); provide a commonly understood framework and vocabulary for planning your business; and help you identify and eliminate waste. These procedures explain what tasks need to be done, who is responsible, and how they relate to each other. They don't, however, provide detailed instructions on how to perform the tasks. Since they don't actually explain how to perform an activity, high-level procedures tend to be most often used at the management level, when you need to understand how processes fit together. The relationships between higher- and lower-level processes can also be used to show employees how their own tasks fit into a bigger whole, which can help them work more intelligently and expand their knowledge of the business.

High-level procedures are built around a process map, but they also contain more information:

- A brief introduction summarizing what the process is and who the intended reader is

- The scope and goals of the process

- Roles and responsibilities, such as who is responsible for what tasks

- What metrics are collected (often called Key Process Indicators, or KPIs)

- What records are kept

- Usually, text explaining the tasks, wherever necessary to provide more clarity than a process map flowchart alone can furnish, and detailing key process inputs and outputs

- References to related higher- and lower-level documents (parents and children)
- Information about the procedure document itself such as:

  - Owner

  - Unique procedure ID

  - Author

  - Approver

  - Date of last revision

  - Definitions of terms and abbreviations used
  - Revision history

There may be more than one level of a process even at the "what" level, because you're often limited both by what can be shown on one page and what can be easily understood without intense study. For large and complex processes, it may be necessary to show a less detailed overview of the process, then break down each task into more detail before you even get to the "how to do it" level. You can do this within one document, or you can break it up into smaller documents. If you decide to create one large document, try to organize it intuitively so that it's easy for readers of the procedure to understand how parts fit together.

In some cases, you need procedures to control other procedures. If you want to be certified to ISO 9001 or a similar standard, six high-level procedures are specifically required. Even if you are not planning to be certified to a standard that requires them, it's a good idea to strongly consider including these procedures anyway, because they govern the other processes in your system. The six procedures are as follows:

1. A *Document Control Procedure* specifies what your standards, procedures, and other documents look like and how they are governed, including what formats are used and what level of approval is required for each kind of document. You can also include information on where templates are stored and how they can be accessed. Like all other procedures, a Document Control Procedure can be made flexible enough to cover a wide range of cases, without requiring senior management approval for every simple work instruction. (See Chapter 8 for further discussion on how to build flexibility into your procedures.)

2. A *Record Control Procedure* controls how records are kept of your work, including (but not limited to) processes followed and decisions made. It specifies what records are kept, how long they are retained, how they are identified, where they are stored, how they can be retrieved, how they are protected, and when and how they are disposed of.

3. An *Internal Audit Procedure* describes how you conduct your own internal audits—that is, how you verify that your procedures are properly documented, maintained, and followed, with proper records kept. These internal audits are distinct from outside audits conducted by a customer or certifying agent.

4. A *Control of Nonconforming Products Procedure* describes the method of ensuring that a product that doesn't conform to specifications is not used, and that appropriate actions are taken. Don't be misled by the word "product"; if you supply a service, that service is your product and you need to make sure your customers are getting what they contract for.

5. A *Corrective Actions Procedure* is closely related to a Control of Nonconforming Products Procedure, but it can have a wider scope. It describes the actions taken to address problems that have been iden-

tified, including doing a root-cause analysis of the problem, taking corrective action to fix the problem, and verifying that the action succeeded in fixing the issue.

6. A *Preventive Actions Procedure* is very similar to a Corrective Actions Procedure, and the two procedures may be combined into one. This procedure governs the root cause, actions taken, and verification of action to prevent potential issues that have been identified but have not yet occurred. Corrective and preventive actions procedures need to include a scope defining which issues will be addressed, since ISO 9001 does not require a root-cause analysis of every possible problem. For instance, these procedures might address only customer complaints or significant quality issues with the end product.

Defining Low-Level Procedures

Low-level procedures explain *how* to perform the actions in the procedure. They are used for training and for ensuring that people perform standard tasks in the correct way. Thus, they are used mostly by the people who actually execute the procedures.

As with high-level procedures, you may want to have multiple levels of low-level procedures in order to break down complex tasks into more manageable parts. And as with the high-level processes, you can do this either within one document with multiple parts or in separate documents. Whichever you choose, try to keep the organization clear and intuitive.

Remember that people may be trying to follow the procedure while reading it, so don't make them hunt back and forth through the document or dig up many other documents before they can complete one simple task (or part of a task). Think about how they'll be working. If they'll be sitting at a table with a laptop in front of them, you can use hyperlinks to make it easy to navigate to different parts of a work instruction. But if they'll be in a cold and wet environment using a printout, don't force them to leaf back and forth through the pages—maybe with gloves on.

Include pictures as well as diagrams wherever they are useful. In fact, with step-by-step work instructions, you might need only a minimum of explanatory text—just the basics that tell about the procedure: the scope, goals, who wrote it, when it was revised, and so forth.

To clarify: When discussing the "how" level of a process system, the words "procedure" and "work instruction" are sometimes used interchangeably. Everyone seems to have a slightly different definition of these terms. In this book, I use the term "procedure" to refer to any standard documented process, and "work instruction" for the most detailed level of step-by-step instructions. For example, I'd say "procedure" when the instructions say "Use the XYZ machine to cut a piece of metal stock to the dimensions indicated in the technical drawing," and I'd say "work instruction" when the instructions say "Press the red button and wait until the indicator shows 32psi and the green light comes on. Now set the ABC dial to 3.5 and turn the DEF switch to On."

A common problem arises when low-level procedures are written by content experts in headquarters for people to use in the lab, manufacturing facility, or field. Though the experts thoroughly understand the product and the machines and tools to be used, they may not have complete knowledge of field conditions. Furthermore, the very fact that they know their content so well can mean that they don't always write instructions clearly enough for people with less expertise. Therefore, it is critical to have the procedures reviewed by one or more of the people who will actually be following them. If you have people in the field performing processes in locations with differing conditions, ask a few of them to review your procedure to make sure it's feasible for them.

DESCRIBING THE INTERACTION
BETWEEN PROCESSES

Traceability is the vertical relationship among processes. For instance, one high-level procedure could contain eight process steps, three of which require child procedures to explain how to execute them. The output of the parent process is one or more outputs of the child processes (others may just be intermediate outputs that are used by another child process). In contrast, *process interfaces* are horizontal relationships: The output of one is the input to another.

Facilitating Traceability

As mentioned earlier in this chapter, all procedures, except the very top one, should have a parent procedure; that is, one step in the process map of a "parent" is expanded into an entire, more detailed, procedure—the "child." I explained above what should be contained in each process level, but the relationship between the levels is also important.

As we saw earlier in this chapter in Figure 2-3, the top-level process map has a box labeled "Develop new toy." At this top level, it is appropriate to summarize this complicated process in one box. But in order to carry out the process, more detail is needed. However, if the next-level procedure were to contain all the details needed to actually develop a toy, it would be too complicated to read and understand. So we break the tasks down further, to the next lower level.

This is a simple example; there may be more levels within the high-level ("what") and low-level ("how") procedures. Also, bear in mind that, for simplicity, only process maps are shown here. In reality, each process map shown would be just a part (the most important part) of a procedure document.

It is possible to allow a procedure to have more than one parent. One of the considerations when designing a procedure system is whether to allow this. In my opinion, you should always carefully consider assigning a procedure to more than one parent. Having a need to assign more than one parent might be a sign that the parent processes can be arranged more logically or more clearly so that multi-parenting isn't necessary. On the other hand, it can also be a sign that you're working efficiently.

Let's say that Wayne's company manufactures and supports complicated patient-monitoring devices used in hospitals. He is creating a procedure for stocking spare parts. The problem is that at some field sites, the engineer is responsible for ordering a new part when he takes one from stock, while at other sites, the logistics department monitors the number of spare parts on hand and uses just-in-time methods to predict when it will need more. Therefore, Wayne concludes that his ordering process has two parents: the Field Engineering Repair process and the Logistics Part Management process. Wayne may be able to agree with his process's stakeholders to create a single line of traceability through the processes.

One solution would be to institute one standard method across the company. If it's not desirable to do that—because of differing customer needs, level of site activity, or regional conditions—Wayne could get stakeholders to agree that the logistics department has the responsibility, even though at some sites it chose to delegate it to engineering. Then he could go on to document the ordering process itself, noting who has responsibility for which steps, and the Field Engineering Repair process could just say, "Under [insert applicable conditions], refer to Logistics Part Management procedure #123, Parts Ordering, to order replacement spare parts." (See the discussion "Keeping It Flexible" in Chapter 8 for more discussion of how to do this.)

Here's another example:

Senrya owns some sales processes in her home warranty company. She realizes that though the company uses completely different procedures to acquire new customers and to maintain relationships with old customers, every year, her company goes through and updates Customer Information Sheets for all current and prospective customers. Therefore, if she creates a documented procedure for the sales department to perform its annual update of the Customer Information Sheets, it could have parents in both the New Customer Acquisition and the Customer Relationship Management procedures. In this case, it clearly makes the most sense for the procedure to have two parents.

Each procedure could have zero, one, or more child procedures, as needed. It is probable that all process chains do not need the same number of levels. In some cases, the highest-level procedure may be simple enough that the only child procedures it needs are specific work instructions. In other cases, where more complex processes are documented, you may need a high-level procedure, another few child procedures that are still high-level (describing "what" needs to be done rather than "how"), and possibly a few lower-level ("how") procedures.

In this way, you can trace from your top-level business overview down to the most specific work instruction. This has a number of advantages. If you cannot figure out the parent of an existing process, that tells you that you're overlooking some area in the next level up, perhaps even in your top picture of the business—or perhaps even that the process you're looking at is not needed and can be abolished. If you have a relatively high-level procedure or a complex one with no children, ask yourself if it needs some. The answer may still be "no," but then it's a considered no and not an oversight.

Establishing Process Interfaces

The difference between parent–child relationships in procedures and horizontal relationships among procedures on the same level lies in the inputs and outputs. Procedures on the same level may be related in that the output of one forms the input of another. In contrast, child procedures exist to explain how parent procedures produce their outputs.

Horizontal relationships among processes can be many-to-many: One process may draw its inputs from one or more "supplier" processes, and its outputs may be inputs for one or more "customer" processes. (I use the words "supplier" and "customer" here to refer to the relationship among processes only—I'm not implying that they belong to your corporate suppliers or customers!) Also, one single input may come from any one of several other processes, and one output may go to one of several other processes.

Consider a simple metal bracket used in other machines: It might be produced by an in-house manufacturing process or purchased from a vendor via a purchasing process. Similarly, if it's produced in-house, it may go on to be used in many different machines, or it may undergo different finishing processes depending on its intended uses.

As noted earlier, one function of documented procedures is to serve as interface agreements between company divisions, departments, processes, and teams. As you plan out or revise your process system, consider the links—inputs and outputs—among your processes. These let you know when you are missing a process that needs to be added or when you have one you don't need. There may also be cases where you find ways to simplify your system or make it more logical by changing procedure boundaries; by combining or splitting procedures; or by re-scoping, changing what is included within one procedure.

Consider where your process inputs come from for each procedure. If you need a process input that isn't supplied by another process or an external supplier, your process cannot succeed. If you have a procedure with an output that isn't being used, either by another internal process or by an external customer, you're wasting your time creating it. You may be able to streamline or even eliminate your process, which would avoid unnecessary work. Documenting a process properly brings stakeholders together to discuss their expectations of each other and agree on who owns what tasks. This is a way to avoid redundancy, but it can also help to break down "siloing," in which lack of communication leads to inefficiency and rework.

It's good to draw out the hierarchy of your procedures in advance to allow you to plan and track the work. However, if you stick to the plan rigidly, you may end up with a nonfunctioning system. Expect the interrelationships of your procedures to change as you write them. If you are first filling in a process system, get your process owners together periodically to review the whole chain of procedures, not just each individual one. You may also find the horizontal relationships changing. Sometimes you can make a process cleaner by moving its boundaries, changing where one procedure stops and another starts.

If nothing at all is changing in your process hierarchy as you create a bunch of new procedures, you should probably get a little worried: Are you asking the right questions? It's a good idea to get the key people working on related processes together, to align on their inputs, outputs, KPIs (more on those in Chapters 8 and 11), and process scope. That way you can check for gaps or overlap between processes.

CHAPTER 3

Creating an Environment in Which to Build Your Procedures

THE TWO MAJOR PARTS of a process system are the *process structure*, which tracks the hierarchy and relationships among procedures, and the *process environment*, which allows you to create, publish, and (optionally) launch procedures. It's much easier to use procedures when they have a standard look and feel, so that you know where to check for the information you need. This also makes it easier for process creators, allowing them to reserve their creativity for the content, where it counts, rather than having to figure out the best format each time. In addition, the process environment contains tools for process mapping and documenting the procedure, as well as for making procedures easily available to users (generally via a corporate webpage). You definitely need a minimum of configuration control to make sure that the users of the procedures can access the most current version as well as to ensure that only one person can change a procedure at a time. You may also want to use software that tracks changes to procedures, in case you need to consult the history or examine a previous version. Finally, you may choose to design standard ways to launch and monitor procedures in operation.

CREATING TEMPLATES FOR STANDARD PROCEDURES

In creating your process system, you need templates for your standard procedures. Templates save you time and energy on both ends: Procedure authors don't have to spend time thinking about how to organize their information, and process users know where to look in the procedure to find the information they need because it's organized the same way every time.

Templates need to be easy to fill out and flexible. Make them easily adaptable for all likely cases and suitable for use at all process levels. Use *Rule S*, and try to keep them as simple as you can, focusing on content rather than lots of unnecessary empty standard verbiage. Don't include information that is not needed, and make sure the formatting doesn't take up all the space. (Headers and footers that are too big can leave little room for important text.)

I recommend that you view your templates as a guideline, not a straitjacket. The goal of a template is to make your people's work easier. If they are spending a lot of time trying to fit information into a package that is the wrong shape for it, you're not achieving that goal. A process that has been contorted to fit a template that doesn't work for it is also likely to be more difficult to use. One way to deal with this is to make your templates flexible. Consider which sections are needed every time and which ones can be optional. You can also make different sections mandatory for different types of procedures; for instance, perhaps all of your manufacturing procedures need a "safety rules" section, which is not relevant for office procedures. You can choose to create different templates for different uses, or a single template with some information marked "Optional" or "Required only for _____."

Think about what information is needed. Do you want the same format for all higher- and lower-level procedures, or do you need a few different types? Can work instructions consist of only a process map, instructions, or a checklist? Even if some "procedures" do consist of only a checklist, you need some minimum background information about each one:

- Title

- Summary description (this can be very short, but when you look at a document, you need enough information to tell what document it is)

- Date of last revision

- Name of person who approved it (the process owner)

- Author (or process owner)

- Any information needed by someone who wants to revise it (e.g., filename; this might not be needed if your process system is set up so that it's obvious)

All this information can go on the title page, or in a title block if you have something like a checklist that doesn't need a separate title page.

For procedures more complicated than a work instruction, in addition to the items above, you also need:

- Goals

- Scope

- Process map (This may need its own template. Consider what symbols you want to use. Also, do you want to include "swim lanes" [discussed in detail in the section "Swim Lanes" in Chapter 7]?)

- Text explaining process steps in more detail (This needs to be a section on the template, but it can be optional, to be omitted if more explanation is not required for a process.)

- Roles (In other words, who is responsible for performing each step in the procedure? This can also be included within the process map. One common method is RACI. [This is discussed in the section "Establishing Roles and Responsibilities Within the Process" in Chapter 7.])

- List of abbreviations and acronyms used in the document

- Definitions of any unusual terms or jargon used

- List of references or documents that process users might need to look at for more information (Again, this may be omitted if there aren't any.)

- Record retention policy (What records need to be kept for this process, where, in what format, and for how long?)

Other items that are not always needed in a procedure template but that could be useful include:

- Parent procedure

- Child procedure(s)

- Revision history (if it is not kept in your document management tool)

- List of risks that might impact the functioning of this process, and measures in place to mitigate those risks

- List of reviewers of the procedure (the people who provided feedback to the author and agreed on the final version of the procedure)

- Key Process Indicators (KPIs) by which the process will be measured (See Chapter 11 for a detailed discussion on choosing KPIs. [If you decide to include these, it is better not to include too many details, so that you can upgrade target values or fine-tune how a KPI is computed as you reevaluate your procedure's operation over time.])

You don't have to make a template from scratch. Apply *Rule R*, and see if you can find examples of procedure templates online or from other companies you deal with (or use the one in the Appendix of this book). Then apply *Rule C* to make it fit your business.

PUBLISHING PROCEDURES AND MAKING THEM USABLE

Once procedures have been created, you need a standard way to control them, make them accessible to their users, and manage them. Later in this chapter, I discuss some of the tools to help with this, but essentially, your process environment needs to incorporate five controls and capabilities:

1. Allow procedures to be published only once they've been approved by the proper people. You need to decide who the proper people are, which may vary for procedures at different levels. Is it enough for a procedure to be approved only by its owner, or does it need to be approved by the next-level manager? Do you want a central process or quality organization to review each procedure? (If so, I recommend requiring this only for high-level procedures and those that affect multiple departments; otherwise, you're setting up more red tape than you probably need.) Also, who will approve cross-department procedures to make sure they are acceptable for all users?

2. Store procedures in a way that makes them easily accessible to all users and stakeholders and that ensures that users see the latest official and approved version.

3. "Lock" procedure files, so that only one person can edit a procedure at a time.

4. (Optional) Provide a standard way to launch new procedures. You may not need this if you have only a few procedures or if they don't change often. However, if you have a lot of changes, your users can get very annoyed when it seems like they're told to change their way of working every other day. It may help if you can develop a batch system, where you launch several changes at once in predictable intervals via standard communication channels, so that users don't feel they're being continually bombarded.

5. (Optional) Provide a reporting methodology so that the appropriate people can see procedure KPIs and take action as needed. You may choose to handle this separately for each procedure, but it's a good idea to have a standard format of reporting for at least the critical procedures. This facilitates communication among management and stakeholders because everyone uses a common reference and understands how to read the data.

REVIEWING PROCEDURES PERIODICALLY

No business is entirely static, nor should your procedures be. Thus far, we have discussed process systems as though they were static snapshots, and all you had to do was figure out what procedures were needed today. However, there will be times when your company wants to add a new capability, and you will need to create a new procedure to match. Of course, there will be times as well when something is going wrong or when a new opportunity is glimpsed and you need to revise an existing procedure accordingly. Experience shows that there will also be times when the business changes slowly, and though no actual problem is noticed, one or more procedures no longer fit existing conditions.

For these reasons, general practice is to review *all* procedures after a set period, usually two or three years. If you follow a standard such as ISO 9001, this review may be required. If not, it's a good idea anyway. It may be that no change is needed, other than a record of the review, but especially in fast-moving companies you often find that the business has changed under you, terminology or technology has moved on, and updates are required.

DECIDING WHICH METHODOLOGIES AND TOOLS YOU NEED

Methodologies are available to guide you through process improvement and even to help you figure out what content your company needs. There are also purpose-built tools on the market that claim to automate various aspects of procedure creation and use. In this section, we examine some of these methodologies and tools.

A Few Possible Methodologies

You need to know about two available methodologies: CMMI and process maturity, and Lean Six Sigma. Even if you do not subscribe to either complete methodology, you may find some of their concepts helpful.

CMMI and Process Maturity

Capability Maturity Model Integration (CMMI) provides a way of determining which procedures are required for a given type of business and of assessing how good those procedures are. In order to better understand CMMI, let's focus first on process maturity, its underlying idea. *Process maturity* is a way to rank process systems, from "chaotic and ad hoc" to "there are processes for some things and we mostly follow them" to "we have all our processes documented and we continually optimize them in response to real data."

CMMI was originally a joint effort of the U.S. Department of Defense, members of industry, and Carnegie Mellon University's Software Engineering Institute (SEI) to standardize and systematize a model of process maturity. As the participation of the SEI implies, CMMI was originally designed for software development processes. It was later expanded to systems engineering processes, and then to product development, service, and acquisition organizations. CMMI has since been spun off from the SEI and is now run by a separate organization, the CMMI Institute at Carnegie Mellon.

CMMI is a recognized standard with its own assessment method, but even if it's not worth it for your business to get assessed, there are two major ideas that you may find very useful.

Process Areas CMMI uses two representations, Continuous and Staged. In the *Continuous representation*, each defined Key Process Area (KPA) is ranked according to whether it's Incomplete, Performed, Managed, or Defined. There are three versions of CMMI, for Product Development, Service, and Acquisitions organizations. In this book, I mostly discuss the form and generic content of procedures rather than offer advice about which ones you need because it varies with your business. You may find it helpful, though, to look at the KPAs for your type of business in order to spark your thoughts about what processes are necessary for your company. You can find these and other CMMI documents on the Institute's webpage, at http://cmmiinstitute.com.

Process Maturity The *Staged representation* ranks all of a company's processes (and process system) together, using the following five defined levels:

1. *Level 1: Initial.* Processes are ad hoc and there is no system. Firefighting is common and rewarded; successes typically come at the price of heroic overwork.

2. *Level 2: Managed.* Processes exist and are followed, and status is reported to management at defined milestones.

3. *Level 3: Defined.* Processes are standardized; in terms of this book, a process system exists that provides standards, procedures, tools, and methods. Standard processes are tailored to each project according to tailoring guidelines, and procedures are typically described more rigorously than in Level 2.

4. *Level 4: Quantitatively Managed.* Processes are measured to determine their performance relative to quantitative objectives; statistical analysis is used to make project and process performance predictable.

5. *Level 5: Optimizing.* Processes are continually improved in order to better meet business objectives and performance needs. There is a quantitative understanding of process variation.

Getting assessed by CMMI and using its whole methodology is a big commitment, one worth doing only if it provides a competitive advantage. Many businesses have found that improvements made with the CMMI methodology have greatly improved their efficiency, effectiveness, and quality level. On the other hand, it's definitely *not* worth getting assessed unless your company is dedicated to making the systemic improvements that will yield real benefits. Even if you need to start by making improvements on a smaller scale, however, it's worth taking a look at the CMMI website, because the main documents are free and CMMI concepts can be useful to you even without a formal assessment.

Lean, Six Sigma, and Lean Six Sigma

Lean Six Sigma is a combination of two methodologies. Both were originally developed to improve manufacturing processes and then were adopted in other business areas. *Lean,* which is based mostly on the Toyota Production System, seeks to minimize waste. *Six Sigma,* which was originally developed at Motorola, seeks to minimize variation in order to reduce defects in the final product. ("Sigma" is a symbol for standard deviation in statistics; a six sigma process is one in which 99.99966 percent of the products manufactured are statistically expected to be free of defects, yielding only 3.4 defects per million.) Since businesses typically want both efficiency and quality in their products, Lean and Six Sigma tools are often used together, and the combination is referred to as *Lean Six Sigma.*

The heart of Six Sigma is an expansion of the familiar Deming cycle, Plan-Do-Check-Act, developed by renowned statistician W. Edwards Deming. Six Sigma takes that cycle a step further into the DMADV and DMAIC methods, whose initials stand for the steps in each method.

For creating a new process or product, use *DMADV*:

- *Define.* Ask the following questions: What are the process goals and scope? Who is on the team? What improvements are you hoping to make?

- *Measure.* Develop quantifiable requirements from customer needs and process goals.

- *Analyze.* Examine design alternatives and the capabilities of design choices.

- *Design.* Create and optimize the detailed design. You may want to use simulations to see how well the process works.

- *Verify.* Confirm that the design meets requirements, set up pilot runs, implement the changes, and check to see whether the procedure meets the goals. Make further improvements, if necessary. Finally, if the process has been created by a different team from the people who will own it on an ongoing basis, hand it over to the owners.

For improving an existing process, use *DMAIC*:

- *Define.* Begin by agreeing on the problem you want to fix. Examine customer needs and determine process goals.

- *Measure.* Collect data on the current situation.

- *Analyze.* Analyze the data to find opportunities for improvement.

- *Improve.* Detail and implement the process improvement.

- *Control.* Create and implement control mechanisms to watch and continually monitor process metrics to make sure the change works as desired.

Various Lean Six Sigma tools are used throughout these phases to find, quantify, and remove waste and process variation.

The rest of this book loosely follows the DMADV/DMAIC methodologies. Chapter 6 discusses how to *define* the problem and *measure* and *analyze* the situation and the customer needs. Chapter 7 and Chapter 8 discuss how to *improve* an existing procedure or *design* a new one by creating/revising and implementing procedures. Chapter 11 is largely based on the Six Sigma idea of needing to *verify* or *control* changes. In addition, a few of the Lean Six Sigma tools, such as SIPOC,

Thought Process Maps, process maps, and control plans, are described in detail in this book.

A Few Possible Tools

When selecting tools to use with your process system, remember this one rule: Always decide on your requirements *first*. Figure out what you want to do, and then select tools that can help you do it. If you select tools and let them guide your way of working, you will end up with unmet or half-met requirements, and your system and processes will never work as well as you hope they will. Of course, some minor aspects of your system have to be driven by tooling. For instance, some tools used for procedure documentation may dictate the documentation's look and feel. However, these tools should not compromise the content you want to have in your processes or the way they link together. Remembering *Rule R*, you may find that some tools are designed to incorporate and provide the benefits of standard wisdom in your field. But balance that with *Rule C* and do not select a tool that won't allow you to customize your system in accordance with your own needs.

Basic Tooling Requirements

The basic tools needed to document a procedure are a word processor and a drawing program. Many companies create their procedures with nothing more than Microsoft Word and Visio or equivalents. (A hint: You can also draw up most process flows using only Excel or PowerPoint. This may facilitate sharing and review of the process, if everyone does not have a license for Visio or whatever drawing program you're using.)

In order to control procedures, you also need some kind of database to store the latest version of the procedure. Safeguards should be in place to make sure that the latest version is always maintained, that only people with the authority to change the procedure can alter the file, and that only one person can work on the file at a time. The simplest way to do this is to have a folder controlled by someone with a gatekeeper role who performs all of these functions manually. However, especially when many people will be working on procedures in your system, it is easier and more effective to use one of the many process library/document configuration control products on the market.

Finally, you need a delivery system that allows people to access the procedures for use. This can be the company intranet. Your database needs to store the procedures in a read-only format (PDF is the most common one) so that everyone on your intranet can pull up the procedure they need to see.

In general, your procedures should be either non-confidential (anyone can see them) or company confidential (any employee or subcontractor can see them, plus possibly some other designated people, such as trusted suppliers). There may be a few cases in which you need to keep your procedures secret (only people who have a "need to know" can see them), as with some human resources, finance, or legal procedures. If you do have any secret procedures, your intranet or other delivery system must be able to control who can view a procedure.

Tools on the market change rapidly, so I am not recommending any specific tooling in this book. I do discuss some of the types of tools available, though, and what they can do to help implement and improve your process system.

Mind Mapping Tools

Mind mapping tools are useful in the brainstorming phase of a project. You can use them to capture all the ideas a team has about what to include in the process, what the risks are, the scope, limitations, and so forth.

The Six Sigma version of this, called a *Thought Process Map (TPM)*, focuses on collecting all the questions that need to be answered in the course of a process improvement project. The idea here is to focus specifically on questions so that you don't jump to solutions before you fully understand the problem.

To create a TPM, get a cross-functional group of stakeholders together and start with a central question such as, "What should this process do?" Write the question on a whiteboard or in a mind mapping tool. Then write down all the questions that central question sparks, and then all the questions those queries spark, until you have a big network of topics to include as you move through the process creation or improvement. (It is possible to just document the questions as a list in a word processor, but using a graphic format can make the thought progression easier to see and can spark further ideas.) If you already know the answers to any of the questions, note those down too for future reference, but in the early phase, try to stay focused on questions. You can keep checking back with the TPM throughout the project, adding new questions as they arise and seeing if old ones have been addressed.

Figure 3-1 shows a simple TPM, but it's a good start on general questions to ask about a new or improved process. Examining this TPM will prompt you to think of many more specific questions.

FIGURE 3-1 A Thought Process Map

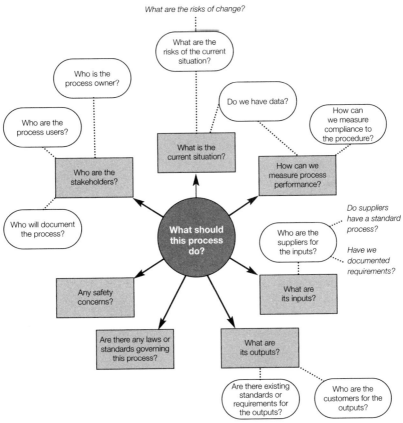

Process Modeling Tools

Any drawing tool can be used to create a process map, but purpose-built tools can make the job easier. At a minimum, a basic tool, such as PowerPoint, provides built-in flowchart shapes, as well as the ability to draw links from one process step to another that stay attached as you move shapes around. Additional capabilities can include swim lanes (rows or columns for each role, so you can see who does what task) and even an automated layout (so that the tool can figure out how to logically organize the process steps). This can help minimize the confusing crossings of links between process steps and can also help you fit the diagram into a compact space. (A surprisingly difficult part of drawing a process map can be making it small enough to include in a procedure document.)

More powerful tools can provide the capability to do graphic process modeling. These tools allow you to drag and drop process objects (steps/actions) and attach business rules that force decisions to be taken in a proper way. Rules can be added or adjusted to quickly adapt to changes in business conditions. These tools typically use a standardized programming language, such as Business Process Modeling Notation (BPMN) or XML Process Definition Language (XPDL), to allow process definitions to be shared between different tools.

These tools also allow you to run simulations to assess how well a process will work under different conditions, so that you can change and optimize your process before going live.

Finally, some process modeling tools provide guidance and reporting as you execute the process. These can offer business rules at the right time to direct your decisions, record when an action has been taken, and track process adherence and performance.

Process Library Tools

Process library (storage, configuration management, and delivery) tools maintain a process library and provide configuration control. They ensure that the procedure your users can see is always the latest version, and they control who can change a procedure. Generally, configuration management tools do this by allowing only one person at a time to work on a procedure. Checking out a procedure from the library produces a writeable version in which changes can be made, while checking it back in promotes that changed procedure to be the official current version. Process storage tools may also automate the approval flow, sending it to each approver in turn and tracking each approver's electronic signature.

Finally, delivery/publishing tools publish the procedure to the intranet so that your users can access them (generally in read-only versions). Some may also provide a way for users to comment on procedures so that their feedback can be used for further improvement.

Any configuration management tool provides for some sort of process number or unique identifier for each stored procedure. Depending on how the tooling is defined, a meaningless number can be assigned to each new procedure or you may be able to set up your own system in which the identifiers have meaning—that is, the numbering system can show how processes are related so that, for example, a high-level process in a manufacturing department might be M1009, one of its low-level child processes could be M1009.3, and the "grandchild" work instruction would be M1009.3.1. If you set up such a system, be sure that it allows for expansion—because you are certain to need it.

Some process library tools may be able to produce a diagram showing the relationship of procedures. This can be very useful for understanding your process hierarchy.

Sticky Notes (The Old-School Method)

Of all of the various tooling aids for process mapping on the market today, the most useful, hands down, is the humble sticky note. In the course of this book, I recommend sticky notes for several purposes. They're extremely beneficial, for example, when you're working with a group to try to pin down exactly what steps are in a given procedure or what procedures are needed in your process system. One situation in which sticky notes are helpful in developing your process system is when you gather a group of people together to figure out what procedures you need to include and how they fit together.

Here's the way it works. Gather together a bunch of stakeholders: management, technical experts, and other people with good knowledge of your company processes. (You may find it more useful to gather different groups of people to flesh out the different parts of your process system, rather than having one group designing the entire system. For example, have manufacturing people determine the manufacturing processes, while salespeople determine the sales processes.) Give everyone a bunch of sticky notes and a pen or a marker, and then allow them fifteen minutes or so to write down all the important processes they can think of. When the time is up, put all the sticky notes on a wall. Next, give the group five minutes, with no talking allowed, to group similar processes, clustering the ones that are alike. Most will be ordered quickly, but there may be areas where a few people are moving the same processes back and forth—identifying areas that require a deeper look. The facilitator can lead a discussion to determine which sticky notes are duplicates, which are aspects of the same process, and which are related processes. You may find that some processes are subsets of other ones. Try to keep your list of processes at the same level for now, but retain the subprocess suggestions for use as you develop the lower levels of your system.

If you have only a few people in the group, let everyone work together. For a larger group, have one person facilitate by going through each sticky note, reading it and then sticking duplicates on top of each other. If there is any possibility of doubt, the facilitator should ask the members of the whole group for their opinion on whether two suggestions are the same.

Finally, the group can put the processes in order, and the facilitator can prompt them to think about what other real-life processes might have been forgotten. Once you're done, it's a good idea to have someone take a picture of the completed process diagram for later reference. (Tip: A smartphone with a good camera is a useful tool to bring to process meetings for this reason.)

CHAPTER 4

Implementing Your Process System

ONCE YOU'VE DESIGNED a complete system, you need to implement it; inadequate implementation is far too common a pitfall. Hopefully, you've made your process system as simple as is practical. This makes it easy to explain the system to process users, process owners, and management. You may need to "sell" the system a bit, because not everyone will immediately understand why it's needed or what it does for the company.

When the system has been implemented, don't assume it's perfect. Check to see if it's working as you expect. Even if it does work perfectly to begin with, the process system may require some tweaks later on, as your company evolves. The last section of this chapter discusses how to tell when a process system needs to be revised. This may also be useful for those who already have an existing process system and don't need to create one from scratch.

GETTING BUY-IN FROM MANAGEMENT

To create a corporate-wide process system, you need support from upper management. According to Gartner's surveys of CIOs, for years, "improving business processes" was among the top ten priorities of CIOs (see www.gartner.com). Interestingly, it dropped off their list in 2012 and 2013. Apparently, processes are no longer trendy. This is not necessarily a bad thing, because good procedures contribute to every one of the items on their lists in any year. Similarly, bad processes can actually detract from, or at least provide no help on, every issue—from attracting customers to reducing costs. (For any year you check, executive goals generally reduce down to a few, stated in different ways: selling more products and services, producing those products and services at lower costs, attracting and retaining the right people. Sometimes goals of moral or environmental responsibilities are added.) To sell a new system to your upper management, you need to convince these people that a process system can link together processes to ensure that they meet the corporate goals, without adding lots of administrative costs.

Even if you already have backing from top management, though, you may get only lip service from managers at the next level who are caught up in operational challenges. This can be problematic, because even if you are able to save them time by using people from outside their departments to document and deploy procedures, you do need time from some of their people to capture the content of their processes and to determine where their processes can be improved. Most likely, the people you need are the very ones who are busiest and most valuable. In order to get more than a few minutes of these people's time, you need to convince both them and their managers of the value of your activities.

In one company, I worked on a process system improvement in which one sector's VP was simply not interested in what we were doing. The project had backing from the company CEO and the board of management, and this VP had been part of a group of senior managers who were given a presentation by the head of the process improvement department. The VP designated one of her people to represent the department, but he hadn't been involved with most of the department's functional processes and didn't really have a process orientation to begin with. After some frustrating weeks—during which we finally gained agreement from the department rep that yes, our model showed his department as he understood it—we were ready to present to the VP. She seemed bored for the first few minutes, but then she grew more interested, and after five minutes she asked, "Have you seen the department plan I wrote?" We hadn't. She asked a more senior person in her department to work with us and to supply that document, and in two weeks we had a better model than we'd previously gotten in two months.

The lesson I learned was: Don't depend on trickle-down directions from the top. Do what it takes to get crucial people on board and to get them to assign the right resources, *before* you spend time trying to extract content information from people who don't have it.

COMMUNICATING IMPORTANT INFORMATION ABOUT YOUR PROCESS SYSTEM

It may seem to go without saying that you need to communicate important information about your system, but apparently it does need to be said because it gets overlooked surprisingly often: Once you have created or changed your process system, tell people what you've done! Also, tell them how it works. You may have done your best to design an intuitive system, but even though it seems crystal clear to you, it may still confuse people who aren't used to thinking in terms of processes and systems. Everyone in the company needs to know about your process system, though not everyone needs to know the same things:

- Everyone—that is, everyone who has any need to follow a procedure, which is probably everyone at the company—needs a broad understanding of what the process system is for. If you implement a new system or make substantial changes to an existing one, people need to understand why you've changed it. They need to understand how to find and read the procedures they need to do their job. If you want people to feel part of the purpose of the company and not merely workers for a wage, they need to understand how their own procedures can be traced up through their parent procedures on up to the top-level model of the business, so they can see how their own work fits into the whole. Their management needs to make it clear that they are expected to accomplish their own tasks by following the documented way of working. Users also need ways to deal with problems they encounter in their work, so that they're not tempted to just stop using a procedure that isn't working well. They need to know how to find a process owner to propose changes to an existing process, and they need to know what to do if they need to request a new process.

- Process owners, process authors, and core members of the process team need the same knowledge as other employees. In addition, though, they need to understand how your process creation and process library tooling works; how to access writeable versions and edit processes; how to get approvals and make them official; how to deploy new and revised procedures; and how to monitor, control, and improve procedures. Of course, they also need to understand the content of and requirements for the processes they own.

- Managers need to understand the same things as process owners, because many of them own processes or are likely to move into roles where they will own processes. They need to have a deeper understanding of the business values of standard procedures and the workings and benefits of this specific process system, and of their own responsibilities to hold their employees responsible for following relevant procedures. Managers also need to pay attention to the reported KPIs of relevant procedures and to manage according to that data.

You may find some of the information in Chapter 10 to be useful in determining how to deploy the new process system and educate your people on the changes.

KNOWING WHEN A PROCESS SYSTEM REQUIRES IMPROVEMENT

Your company may already have a perfectly good process system in place that doesn't require any changes. If so, when you need a new procedure, you simply have to figure out how it fits into the existing structure. Otherwise, you may be able to improve the existing system rather than create a new one.

How do you know when your process system is in need of improvement? We've already discussed what to do when you don't have a process system at all (in Chapter 2). One step beyond that is the situation in which you have a process inventory that is simply a list with no indication of hierarchy or how procedures relate to each other. That's not a real system: It doesn't help you see where you have gaps or wasted effort. In this case, you need to figure out how your processes relate to each other so that you can see whether any are missing or redundant. Also, you must determine whether there is a process environment, with an established way to create and publish procedures.

A common situation is one where a system does exist and is widely understood but is not written down. This might seem easy to fix because you only need to document what already exists, but it's likely that people have different understandings without realizing it. In that case, you need to facilitate discussions to get people to come to a common understanding so that the system can be documented in a way that meets everyone's expectations. Don't assume that your own understanding of a process system is correct and universal. Instead, write down your idea of it, call in a cross-section of stakeholders, and revise your document until everyone agrees it is correct. With an undocumented system, it's easy to miss some parts: Check to see whether all your procedures are included and, as mentioned above, whether you have a process environment as well as a process structure.

I said previously that if there's already a good process system, you just need to figure out where a new procedure fits into it. If you can't do that because the system doesn't seem to have a place to incorporate the new procedures, that's another sign that it needs improvement. Your system may be out of date, or it may be too rigid and inflexible to encompass your whole business and any future changes. In either case, you need to evaluate it and decide how to revise it. If it's been working well otherwise, only minor changes may be needed.

Finally, you may have a system in place that seems to be OK but is just not working well. This may be so if you see any of the following symptoms:

- Users are not following procedures.

- Procedures are not monitored and improved when needed.

- Procedures are not properly approved.

- Process structure is not being consulted, so gaps exist where there are no procedures for critical processes or redundant procedures are created.

- Procedures are not published properly. For example, procedures may be on department websites or other locations instead of in the normal procedure library.

- Auditors are returning major procedure-related findings or a significant number of minor ones.

- Procedure-related audit findings are not addressed in a timely way.

If you encounter any of these symptoms, or any others that seem to indicate problems with the process system, the first question to investigate is whether the system is at fault or whether people just don't understand it (or know it exists). If people do know about it but choose not to use the system, figure out why. The system may be flawed and hard to use, or they may not understand it. Sometimes good systems are communicated badly; sometimes systems that seem to be good turn out to be unusable in practice, because not enough attention was paid to the needs of the users when the system was developed. A thorough investigation into the root causes of the issues you're seeing, coupled with a good understanding of what a process system ought to be, should reveal what changes need to be made. Try to fix only what's actually broken. It can be tempting to tear the old system down and start from scratch, but that's likely to be a long and arduous project. It will be easier on you as well as on the system's stakeholders and users if you can fix only the broken aspects of the existing system.

A logical process system provides the support your procedures require to stay strong, effective, and connected. As the shape of your business changes over time, keep your process system updated and accurate, so that your procedures can continue to function smoothly.

CHAPTER 5

Managing Your Processes and Process Systems

THIS CHAPTER IS AIMED AT MANAGERS who own a process system or a chunk of one and need to ensure that processes stay in alignment. Later sections of this book have been aimed at the individual contributor—the person in charge of creating or revising a process and making sure that it works. If you are the manager of these people, you need to understand their activities as well. However, you also need to understand the processes and how they work together from a systemic viewpoint. You must be able to set intelligent goals for your team and make sure their processes are rolled out in a coordinated way. After their processes have been rolled out, you need to be able to review the process operation to ensure that the processes are working as planned. This chapter addresses those big-picture questions for anyone who is in charge of multiple processes that function together in a system.

You may be working with people who are inexperienced at writing and implementing processes or who do not take a process-based view of work and don't want to spend time "creating red tape instead of doing real work." (Of course, you could just lend them this book!) In that case, as you seek to develop a process-based mentality throughout your organization, you're doing change management, and I recommend that you use both top-down and bottom-up channels. One bottom-up channel for change is helping people to understand why a process is needed. For one thing, if the way of working is explained in a clear document that's easy to access, then people will not need to bother their more experienced coworkers for guidance as often. A top-down channel for change is making sure that the process tasks are part of your team's workload, not an addition on top of an already overcrowded workday. These process tasks should be included in the employee's individual evaluation goals, and you should follow through by prioritizing tasks such that the work can get done. Relating a task to next year's appraisal is a powerful motivator for employees, and prioritizing process work over some other tasks forces managers to give more than lip service to process improvement. (See Chapter 13 for additional ideas on driving change through your organization.)

Of course, there is no one right way to make your team effective. In this book, I discuss some methods that have worked well in actual practice, but, as always, you need to make judgments based on your own people and company culture.

MAINTAINING THE BIG PICTURE

Process owners are responsible for the content of their own processes. With wider awareness, they can also work together to maintain horizontal and vertical relationships among processes. The owner of a child process is responsible to the owner of a parent process for making sure that his process is consistent with the parent, and he is also responsible for aligning with the owner of a related process on the same level to make sure the outputs of one process are used as inputs by at least one other process.

The problem here is that owners of lower-level processes don't always know about all processes that relate to their own, especially when new processes have been added. That's why the system is important, to track the relationships among all the processes. When a good system is in place, a process owner simply needs to look at the charts of the system, from the top-level business process model on down through the process maps in procedures going down the hierarchy, to see where his own process fits in.

Someone needs to be responsible for understanding the big picture, seeing how these processes fit together, and keeping them up to date and consistent with each other. That someone is the owner of the high-level processes, who thus has authority over the whole system or a chunk of it. This responsibility can be delegated if the manager doesn't have time to do it, but in that case (as with any time responsibility is delegated), sufficient authority needs to be delegated along with the responsibility, in order to make sure that the person in charge can be effective. To make the relationships clearer, it's good practice to reference a procedure's parent and child procedures.

When doing this, you may want to keep diagrams of the process maps in your area so you don't have to keep looking inside each procedure to see the process hierarchies. If you do print out the diagrams, be careful to keep them up to date—there's the risk that procedures will change, rendering your diagrams outdated. However, if done properly, these diagrams will not change often since they show only the relationships.

TRACKING CHANGES IN PROCESS RELATIONSHIPS

Thriving companies are rarely static—there are endless books on the increasing pace of change and how to deal with it. As your business environment, corporate culture, and customer demands evolve, your procedures evolve with them. I've already mentioned the idea of regular periodic review of processes. However, other times procedures need to be updated because of major changes in the business. This is why it's important to maintain your process system. If you know which engineering processes require inputs from or provide outputs to finance processes, for example, then when there is a major change within the work of the engineering department, you'll know if any finance processes need evaluation to see if revision is required. Sometimes immediate change is needed, but many times you may find that the change is small enough that the affected process can be allowed to remain as it is until the next time it needs revision anyway. (It can be very helpful if your process library system has a way to attach a note to a procedure, specifying the changes needed in future updates.)

When major changes do affect more than one process, it might be a good idea to get your process owners together to review not only the processes themselves but also the links between them. In this way, you can find gaps where a new process needs to be created, or overlaps where one task shows up on more than one process and you have too many stakeholders. Eliminating the overlap may require changing the scope of one or more processes. Even without overlap, you might find that you want to move one part of a process to another to make it cleaner, changing where a process starts and stops; sometimes slight changes to the sequence or ownership of activities or child procedures can improve process efficiency.

MANAGING MULTIPLE SIMULTANEOUS PROCESS IMPROVEMENT INITIATIVES

There are many cases when you might need to oversee several process improvement initiatives at once for related processes. This can happen when you're setting up a new company, building a new process system in a company that didn't really have one before, or adding a major new capability that requires many new processes. You may also find that a new plant requires new processes, even though it's doing essentially the same activities as existing plants, because of unique organizational structure, issues of scaling, or cultural or regulatory factors. One company moved a factory from Europe to Asia and realized that it needed multiple new procedures for two reasons: The existing procedures were written in the local language rather than in the official corporate language, and the way in which the procedures were written assumed that process users were very experienced. This wasn't true of most workers in the new factory, so the processes had to be revised to be easier for them to use.

Managing multiple interrelated process improvements at one time poses special challenges and requires program management skills. You need to keep project schedules in line so that information about one process is there when it is needed by another, even though some of the interlocking processes may not be known in much detail yet. Fortunately, you don't need to know the inner details of processes to link them together, only the outer shell—their scope, inputs, and outputs. (Anyone who has worked on object-oriented software is familiar with this idea.)

In Part 3, I talk in detail about how to create or revise a procedure. In short, though, you begin by defining the procedure's goals and scope, what you have going into it and what you need to get out of it. Once you have defined these for each procedure, at least in a rough draft, you know enough to begin developing them further, though the teams working on each one still need to stay in contact to make sure they're aligned as they determine process inputs and outputs in more detail. One way to do this is to have a single person (an overall manager or a delegate) involved in defining these basics for all related procedures. An even better idea is to define the fundamentals of the related procedures together at one time, in a workshop with all project leads or entire teams present. Sometimes this leads to tough discussions on who owns what and what the particular requirements are for specific inputs and outputs. As the discussion evolves, you can change the scope of the procedures in relation to each other to set the boundaries at the points that make transitions simple.

For an example of what I mean by "simple transitions," let's say you are developing manufacturing procedures for a company that makes hanging lamps. The light assembly and controls for several of your models are identical, but because the glass covers are shaped differently, some pointing up and others pointing down, the attachment points from the lighting assemblies to the shades need to be different. You can have one standard procedure to make the internal lighting assembly and then include the manufacture of the connections in the separate procedures governing each cover style. That way, you don't need a bunch of procedures for the lamp covers and a bunch of procedures for the lighting assembly with each different connector. Forever after, whenever you have a new lamp style, you can just design it to attach to that one standard lighting assembly.

It is good practice to have process creators name a new procedure, register it in your process library, and get its unique number as soon you and your group have identified what procedures will be created. This way, interlinking procedures can reference each other and work can be done in parallel. Once the name and identifier of a procedure are known, other procedures can refer to it.

Let's say you are creating a bunch of new processes and you get the process creators together to align their interfaces. You find that the links between processes are not changing at all. Maybe, then, you should worry a bit. Are you asking the right questions? Do you have the right people in the room? Check process inputs, outputs, KPIs, scope, and initiation and termination points. Make sure there are no gaps or over-laps and no duplication of records or activities. From the users' point of view, is the organization logical, or will it make them go to two or more processes to get their work done?

As I mentioned earlier, the relationships among processes often change as the processes themselves are fleshed out. Sometimes writing out a procedure makes it clear that the process is too complex. In this case, you have a few choices. You can divide the tasks up into more than one process, but that might not make sense. You can also make it a parent process, by omitting detail in the main process and adding some lower-level processes in which the detailing is defined. This detailing can then be handled by the team working on that process, assuming their workloads allow it; otherwise, you need to assign more resources.

FIGURE 5-1   Status of Processes for a New Factory

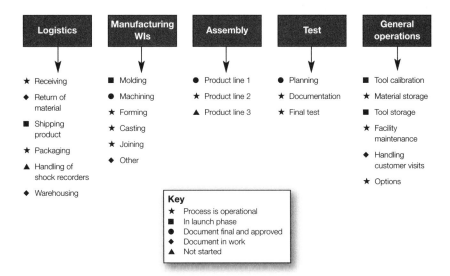

You may find it useful to create a diagram showing the status of your processes, using colors, patterns, or symbols to indicate which ones are done. Figure 5-1 shows the status of processes for a new factory.

It's possible that some of these procedures might have children of their own. If so, this can be shown in a couple of ways. You could decide that the status of the parent procedure is the lowest (furthest from finished) status of itself and all its children, or you could show only the status of each procedure itself and keep a separate chart showing the status of each of its children.

SETTING PROJECT GOALS AND SCHEDULES FOR PROCESS CREATORS

Sometimes processes are created by experienced project managers. In my experience, more often they are created by content experts or designated "project people" who are not used to building and executing a project plan—or else they are just treated as a different kind of work.

As a manager, you need to know what your people are doing and whether their work is being completed on schedule. Therefore, it will be useful to you to work with your team to create a realistic schedule that allows them to report progress accurately. There's more information on how to schedule a process improvement project in Chapter 14, written for the point of view of the project leader, but if you are the manager of those leaders, you need to have status reported regularly so that you are aware of issues before they blow up into bigger problems.

Based on my experience, I have found that many process owners have trouble getting around to creating and implementing a new procedure when they're doing it on top of their operational responsibilities. If you allow three months to get the job done, you often find that not much has been done at the end of that time. Unless progress is reported along the way, much time can be wasted before you even learn that there is a problem. You can avoid this by dividing the work into relatively small and manageable tasks, even if it seems artificial to do it that way. Here's one example of how that can be done:

Allen is a manufacturing manager setting up a new factory for his company in a new country. He is familiar with a process-based approach, but his people are not, and they need to create a whole set of new procedures and work instructions for the new factory. Allen defines and schedules the following tasks for each of his procedure creators, giving them one week to finish each action:

- *First task:* Write the header page and upload it to the document management system, reserving a document number.

- *Second task:* Write a brief introduction, with scope and goals.

- *Third task:* Assemble a team, confirm the process owner, and create the SIPOC, which stands for Supplier-Input-Process-Output-Customer and provides a simple black-box model of a process. (See Chapter 7 for more information on SIPOCs.)

- *Fourth task:* Create the process map.

- *Fifth task:* Have the process map reviewed by Allen and the owners of all linked processes.

- *Sixth task:* Update the process map based on review feedback.

- *Seventh task (and later tasks):* Write a verbal description of each process step, specifically identifying all inputs/outputs, and write the rest of the procedure.

This got momentum going for Allen's team since it's usually easier to continue working on a new project than to start one. The first task seemed easy, but it made the procedure real and got it into the company's configuration management, with a "draft" status. The second task accomplished the work discussed in detail in the first half of Chapter 6. The third task covered the remainder of the work in that chapter and the first part of Chapter 7, providing the information necessary to understand how this process relates to others. The fourth task was to work with the team to envision the process itself. The fifth and sixth tasks incorporated feedback from stakeholders, and later tasks included filling out and completing the procedure. (See Chapter 8 for more details on how to do this.)

Another advantage to breaking down the steps this way was that procedures didn't have to be written by the process owner. In addition to the senior members of his department, who owned and understood the work that needed to be done, Allen also had some people with good communication skills but a bit less technical knowledge. When needed, in order to balance the workload, Allen was able to shift the procedure writing to some of these people, which freed up the process owners to work on other procedures or on operational responsibilities.

Allen's method allowed him to identify lack of progress in time to find solutions, as well as to structure the work for his team, enabling them to be more effective. He was able to see when people needed more coaching and to provide the guidance they needed.

KEEPING YOUR SYSTEM ORGANIZED OVER TIME

To keep a process system working over the long run, you don't need a workshop full of procedure elves who jigsaw all interfaces to fit, but you do need process owners who take their responsibilities seriously. These are often easiest to find for lower-level processes, because it's simpler to see their daily inner workings. When you have a work instruction like "Replace a broken part" or the next level process like "Fix a broken machine" (which could include running diagnostics, replacing the appropriate part, and testing the fix), it's easy to see what's being done or not done and where the process interfaces are. When you get to a very high-level process like "Provide customer support," though, it may include linked processes like "Fix a broken machine," "Perform preventive maintenance," "Order and maintain spare parts," "Train technicians," "Negotiate service contracts," and so forth. Changes in one process can seriously affect another. Here's an example:

Aimee is a service manager in charge of maintaining the milling machines at a customer's site. When her company changed its method of tracking service contracts, she wasn't informed. A machine at a customer's site went down on a Sunday, and she sent the on-call tech out to fix it right away—only to be informed the next day by her manager that the customer in question had not paid for a 24–7 contract, and she should have waited until Monday to have the machine fixed rather than paying overtime rates to the on-call tech. Furthermore, this customer ought to have been billed for the parts used, rather than having them provided for free under warranty.

Fortunately for Aimee's future career, after making a few calls she was able to show her manager that the new method of tracking contracts (which had been developed by the finance department) had never been communicated to her—and indeed, most of the service managers had not been informed that they needed to request accounts on the new system. She and her manager escalated the issue, and the company ended up introducing a new procedure to respond to customers' "machine down" calls. It included steps to check the service contract, schedule repairs accordingly, inform customers of how repairs would be billed, and only then fix the machine. Aimee was included in the planning of the new process, and she was able to ensure that this one was properly deployed to all service managers and techs.

In Aimee's case, the problem did indeed lie in process interfaces. A new method of negotiating and recording service contracts had been developed by the sales department. Sales had conscientiously involved the customer support department's finance team in deciding how to track the contracts, but neither group had remembered that the service contracts also provided important information for the on-site service teams. (If this seems like far too obvious a thing to overlook, I can only respond that while this example is entirely fictional, I have seen equally obvious oversights on the part of large, successful, and normally well-organized corporations. Oftentimes, departments are so focused on excelling in their own work that they forget where it impinges on others.) This is why it's important to have not only defined interfaces between processes but also involved process owners who take their responsibilities seriously. In this case, if contract tracking was documented as part of the overall process of supporting customers, and if the owner of that overall process took an active role in managing it, he should have been notified of the changes and could have alerted the sales team that was making the change of other related processes. Also, leaders of the teams involved could have participated in the rollout of the new process, and they could have monitored the operation of their part of the process to make sure it was effective. In this way, committed process owners can ensure that a robust process system is maintained and kept up to date.

PART THREE

Creating or Revising a Procedure

CHAPTER 6

Planning Your Changes

IN THIS CHAPTER, we discuss how to define your problem, understand the existing situation, and figure out how this process will fit into the process system. It might seem a little frustrating at first, but before you start to actually write a procedure, you need to spend some time figuring out exactly what your procedure needs to do. This will end up saving you a lot of time because it keeps you from realizing midway through that you've just developed a great solution . . . for the wrong problem.

Whenever you want to improve a process (or anything else, really), you begin by defining the problem: What's broken and needs to be fixed, or where is there an opportunity for improvement? Who has the authority to make it work? Next, you investigate the current situation and the needs of all of the process's stakeholders, and from what you've learned you figure out what needs to be changed: Are you going to create a completely new capability, improve the efficiency of an existing process, or what? Then and only then do you make the changes. You have to define the details of the process, write it down, review and revise it until all stakeholders are in agreement with it, then launch it to your users: provide training and whatever tools and infrastructure they'll need to execute the procedure. Finally, you have to continue to manage the procedure's operation by monitoring KPIs and making fixes, changes, and improvements as necessary. (Notice that this loosely matches the DMAIC methodology, as discussed under the heading "Lean, Six Sigma, and Lean Six Sigma" in Chapter 3.)

Another way to look at it is that you begin by considering the process as a part of the larger system: What is it supposed to do, what are its boundaries, what are the major inputs and outputs? Once you're ready to begin writing down the procedure itself, you set down the goals and scope (the boundaries), then figure out the existing situation and what needs to be done to change it. Then you're ready to create the process map, which is the heart of the procedure. You fill in all the details around it, and then finally you review the procedure to see if it's consistent with the boundaries, scope, and goal you defined, and if further improvements can be made.

Note: Within this chapter, I am assuming that you are the project lead and that you are taking on the facilitator role to lead the team in defining the procedure. (See Chapter 12 for further definition of the facilitator role.) However, this section is useful for any team member or manager so that they understand what needs to happen when creating or revising any procedure.

Also note that beginning in this chapter, I introduce an In-Depth Example. I'm going to get a little metaphysical, using the process of process improvement itself as an example, in order to have something that is applicable to any field of business. I develop this example in greater depth and examine it in five parts (the first of which appears at the end of this chapter) during the course of the book, showing how to create and document a standard procedure, launch it into operation, and monitor the procedure to make sure it's running correctly. See Figure 6-1 for the basic steps of a "process improvement process." I am going to focus on the middle box of the figure, "Determine and capture the new / improved process," since that's exactly what we're doing here.

FIGURE 6-1 The "Process Improvement Process"

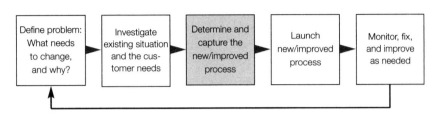

For this initial planning stage, you may be working alone or with very a small team. Don't worry about pulling a complete project team together. For now, it's enough to include yourself and only the people who most obviously need to be included: the owner of the process, if known; your manager, if she has a vested interest in the improvement of this process; and anyone who is directly affected and wants to be included in the process improvement planning. Later on, you will determine who the primary stakeholders are and pull together a process improvement project team. For now, I refer to the people working with you at this point as your project partners, to distinguish them from the later complete team.

MAKING YOUR INITIAL DECISIONS

Before you do anything else, you need to make some basic decisions. These are all aspects of the simple question "What are you trying to do?" These decisions need to be specifically discussed so that you, your team, and your sponsors are all on the same page.

Deciding Which Process You'll Work on First

The first thing to do is to decide which process you're creating or revising. When more than one process needs improvement, you almost always need to balance a number of factors in deciding where to start. Which process is causing the most problems for your company? Where can you have the biggest impact? (These two questions may not have the same answer; reasons outside your span of control may dictate why one process is problematic.) There's also the question of availability: Will the people whose help you need for a given process be available to work with you? In addition, are there any processes whose issues are easily fixed? One process might be easier to fix than another for a number of reasons. Among others, it might have better management backing; it might be performed by people who are more receptive to change; it might impact fewer people or require less tooling; it might be easier to measure accurately; it might be better understood; or it might have users and content experts who are eager to make improvements.

You might want to pluck these low-hanging fruits first, even if they aren't your biggest problems, in order to establish a track record of success that can be used to get management support and to get your people used to a process mindset, if that's something new for them.

If you have a "linchpin" process, whose definition drives many other processes, this is also a good starting point. These are often cross-functional processes, where you need to separate responsibilities among departments or teams managed by different people. However, be warned: Whenever you are working on closely intertwined processes, a change in one procedure may drive a realization that you need to revise related procedures. If you begin by working on the procedure for the central linchpin process, this will reduce these needed changes, but not eliminate them, so you may want to avoid finalizing the linchpin procedure until others close to it are nearly done.

Deciding What Type of Change You'll Make

OK, you've made a decision: You are working on Process X. Congratulations, you've got a process improvement project! Now you need to decide exactly what that previous sentence means—specifically, you need to define the words "You," "are," "working," and "Process X." You get a free pass for "on." (I'm not being silly or needlessly pedantic: Precise meanings are very important when you're creating a procedure. This is very good practice for working on a procedure with a team— over and over you'll find that everyone uses the same words to mean slightly different things and you need to agree on precise definitions in order to have meaningful conversations, in which everyone leaves with the same understanding of what you've just discussed.)

"You" and "are" are pretty easy, to start with. You probably already know your own role in the project—whether you're the project leader, the champion (who delegates other people to do the work and convinces higher management of the project's importance), or a project team member. If you don't have complete authority over the process yourself, you also need a sponsor from a higher level of management. In addition, you may already have a few project partners, as mentioned above. Start working with those people; you can figure out the other team members and stakeholders in a bit. That takes care of the "you" in the sentence "You are working on Process X." As for "are," you might not have a detailed plan yet, but you probably have some idea of when you're expected to begin work and when you're expected to have the procedure in place and running.

But what about that word "working"? Whether there's an existing documented procedure or not, there is probably already a process in place. (The exception is when you are adding a capability that is completely new for your company.) There may be more than one existing procedure, where people doing the same task are doing it in different ways, or there may be an agreed-upon way of working, whether it's documented or not. Is your task to document and standardize an existing way of working, or is it to improve the process, making it more efficient and/or effective? Ensure that you and your management sponsors agree on the goals of your project.

Finally, you need to define exactly what you mean by "Process X." In other words, you need to set up the boundaries of the process.

Determining Your Initial Goals

The first step in defining the process is figuring out your goals. Get yourself and your project partners into a room and agree on these goals, making sure they are worded clearly enough to be understandable to others who are not involved in this discussion. (It may be helpful to prepare an initial set of goals before the meeting. Even if you end up changing it, having an initial draft can spark conversation.) Make these goals as objective as possible and try to phrase them in a way that will make sense in the future, when you've forgotten the details of today's problems and discussions. You really have two sets of goals here: (1) the process improvement project goals (i.e., why you or your management feel the need to improve this process) and (2) the process's own goals. The goals of your process improvement *project* might be an improvement like "Improve bookings by 20 percent." A year from now, you might be looking at different numbers, so this is not the goal you want to build into the process itself. The process's own goals would be something less specific like "Get bookings into the system aggressively and efficiently." Only the process goals will be part of the procedure itself, though project goals can be considered when you later define KPIs to measure the process by and when you set KPI targets (see Chapter 11).

It sometimes happens—when designing a new process, or when documenting and agreeing on a way of working—that the project and process goals are the same. For example, both could be something like "Follow a standard, efficient, and effective way to get bookings into the system."

Project goals are almost always set by internal customers (i.e., management), whereas process goals may be from the point of view of either internal or external customers. Think about the outputs of the process and the required characteristics for those outputs, such as their cost, timeliness, quantity, functionality, and quality. Here are some examples:

- *For a lightbulb manufacturing process:* For your internal customers (management), a project goal might be "to double the current output per month at the same cost per bulb." Meanwhile, for your external customers, a process goal might be "to produce bulbs at high volume and low cost at a level of quality that satisfies the customer." (You can then specify KPIs for such things as how many bulbs, cost per bulb, and average lifetime of each bulb.)

- *For a travel-request process:* The project goal might be "to reduce travel costs to 75 percent of the current level, by eliminating unnecessary travel," whereas the process goal might be "to provide a method that is efficient and easy for users while providing controls to prevent unnecessary travel."

Defining the Scope by
Setting Process Boundaries

Defining the scope is all about setting boundaries: Where does the process begin, why does it begin there, where does it end, and what do you want to *exclude* from this process?

Begin by discussing the start and end. Begin at the beginning: What are the triggers for this process? In other words, how do you know when the procedure needs to be started? Each process has a trigger, and each trigger is unique. Processes can be triggered by time, usage, demand, activity, or a host of other factors. One manufacturing process begins when the previous one is done—for example, the polishing process begins when the machining process ends. An assembly process could begin when all components have been created or acquired, or at a set time based on when the final product must be delivered. A payroll process might run on the first of every month, whereas an aircraft engine is overhauled after a certain number of flight hours, regardless of how much calendar time has passed.

Some processes can have more than one trigger. For instance, a part might be replaced either when the old part breaks or at set intervals during the course of preventive maintenance. This can be simplified by being careful of how you define the scopes of adjoining processes. In this case, you might have one process for investigating the cause of a machine's failure (which would find the broken part) and another one for defining the schedule of preventive maintenance. Then either of those could be followed by the part-replacement process, whose trigger is defined simply as the decision to replace the part.

Next, how do you know when the process is finished? I was once taught a phrase that comes in useful here: "What does success look like?" If the process has been successfully completed, what has changed in the world? Successful completion for a given process might be when a product passes a test, when employees are paid, or when approvals are given for the process outputs. The process should be completed when its goals have been met. If this does not seem to be the case, reevaluate the process goals.

Consider what you want to specifically exclude from the process, and define it as out of scope, as seen in this example:

The Pelner Metrics Company produces customized software products that allow customers to track their own production efficiency and quality. Because Pelner Metrics as a company emphasizes quality, the process owner and project sponsor are excited about creating a new software development procedure that emphasizes forward-looking practices, such as customer participation in requirements reviews and peer reviews of code, in the belief that adding these checks up front will save them time fixing bugs later.

The team is now writing the procedure, and in their enthusiasm, they plan to say that it covers *all* software developed at the company. Then Jim, a team member who is a senior software developer, speaks up. He points out that the company also develops software modules for internal use only, for things like time charging or keeping track of employee capabilities. The team agrees that while the new methodology will be encouraged, they don't want to be that strict about processes for internal software. They write their scope to say: "This procedure covers the development of all software created for sale to external customers."

As you investigate the process, you may learn that you need to change the procedure goals a bit, or to increase, decrease, or move the process scope.

The exact boundaries of a process are usually somewhat arbitrary, especially when you are defining multiple interlocking procedures—where does one begin and the other end? It depends on whose point of view you want to include in the procedure. These decisions also help you determine what triggers the process. For instance, consider the procedure for overhauling an engine on a small Cessna aircraft. If you include the aircraft owner's point of view, the trigger for getting an overhaul is when the owner's logbook shows that the plane has reached 100 hours of flight time since the last overhaul. However, it's more likely that the Fixed Base Operator (FBO) who provides aviation mechanical services only needs to write procedures documenting her own processes. From the operator's point of view, the trigger for performing an engine overhaul is when the customer shows up and says, "I need you to overhaul the engine on my Cessna." As discussed earlier, careful consideration of where to set the boundaries between adjoining processes can simplify the procedure.

Getting Agreement on Who Owns the Process

We've discussed the idea of process ownership, but at the time you begin creating or revising a procedure, that is not always clear—in fact, lack of ownership may be one of the main causes of the problems you're addressing. The proper person to be the process owner is the lowest-level person on the org chart who has enough authority and resources to ensure effective implementation and execution of the project. However, many times this is not the person who is driving the process change. The person who cares enough to want to fix the process may be a customer of the process, or it may be one of the people who is responsible for carrying it out—in other words, the person who feels the pain when a process is not working well or who sees an opportunity for it to work better.

In this case, the person who requests the change needs to identify and work together with the process owner. It's essential that they both understand (at least at a high level) and care about the process. Ideally, effective functioning of the process is one of the criteria by which the process owner's own work is reviewed.

For processes to be carried out within one department, it's not usually that difficult to figure out who should be the process owner. If you are not the owner, you need to get that person (or even better, that person and his manager) on board. You might need to prepare a business case to explain the importance of the process and the opportunities for improvement. You should consider external benefits to the company, such as more sales or bookings, but also include internal benefits, such as better efficiency. Try to include as many quantifiable benefits as possible in addition to the unquantifiable ones, such as improved customer satisfaction or employee morale, because quantifiable improvement opportunities are the easiest for the process owner to sell to his management. (Instructions for generating a business case are not in the scope of this book, but if you need help, there are many excellent books on project management. Briefly, the key components of a business case are expected cost, including resources needed; expected benefits, both quantifiable and not; and time frame over which you expect to achieve the benefits.)

It's generally more difficult to determine the owner of a process that involves multiple departments. Basically, there are three ways to do it, each with its own risks and benefits:

1. Go up the management chain and give the process to the first manager in the hierarchy whose authority spans all departments.

    *   *Pro:* That manager will definitely have the authority to make sweeping changes to the business and will be able to get whatever resources are needed.

    *   *Con:* That manager is likely to be at such a high level that there are many demands on his time, and one process may not be critical enough to get the attention it needs.

    *   *Making It Work:* If the manager cares about this particular process enough to spend time on it, then he can be an effective owner. If not, he can designate someone else to be the functional process owner, giving that person enough authority within all affected departments to make the needed changes.

2. Designate a process owner within one department, while enlisting support from all other affected departments.

    *   *Pro:* This can be someone who has both enough authority and enough bandwidth to actually work on the process.

    *   *Con:* Even with support agreements with the other affected departments, it can be difficult to get the needed resources there, especially if the process owner is not familiar with how things work outside his department.

    *   *Making It Work:* Choose someone with good experience and contacts in the other departments. Make sure that the effective working of the process is something on which all affected de-

partments are monitored. Make sure the process owner has the backing of management of all affected departments or above that of all affected departments.

3. Designate two or more process owners, one from each affected department. This is extremely risky and is mentioned mostly for completeness, because any change would need concurrence from all.

   - *Pro:* Owners are involved with authority and understand all departments involved.

   - *Con:* Management by committee is never a good idea. Even the smallest changes are apt to be cumbersome.

   - *Making It Work:* My best advice is: Don't. However, there are ways to incorporate the advantage of this method into others:

     - Pull in stakeholders from all affected departments and make them key members of the process team.

     - Design the procedure to link together a number of subprocedures, each including the part of the process that falls within a single department, and make sure that the process owner of each subprocedure is within the appropriate department, with the overall process owner taking responsibility for linking them together.

Calling in the Stakeholders and Assembling a Team

Now that you have figured out the process boundaries and have a process owner, it's time to complete your team. You need to include people with the following roles, though it's possible for one person to fulfill more than one of these roles:

- Process improvement project lead

- Process owner (The best case scenario is that the process owner is or has a delegate who is also the project lead.)

- Content experts

- People involved in daily operation of the process (This should be a representative sampling, especially if you have people who will be performing the same process under differing conditions. They might be in different departments or different countries or working with customers who have different requirements.)

- A representative from each affected department (if the process affects more than one)

If the team is larger than three or four people, you may also wish to enlist a trained facilitator if none of the team members has this skill. This helps to make process-planning meetings more effective. (See Chapter 12 for more information on facilitation.)

You may also choose to enlist a technical writer if the process owner doesn't have the time to write the process and has no delegate who can do so. There are disadvantages and advantages to this. A disadvantage of enlisting a tech writer is that it can create less of a feeling of ownership in the process owner. Also, a tech writer who is not an expert on the subject material has to spend much time consulting with the process owner and other experts in order to get the content and terminology right, so schedules become a sticking point. One advantage of enlisting a tech writer is that the procedure documentation may get done faster if it is done by someone whose job is specifically to create documentation rather than by someone who has to make time for it among lots of other responsibilities. Another advantage to using a tech writer is that it may result in a process that is more clearly written, though collaboration means the job is generally slower than if it is done by one person. (If the procedure is written by a content expert, that person is apt to assume that others are as familiar with the process as she is. The content expert needs to be careful to get feedback from people who are less experienced in that area in order to ensure clarity.)

You need a process champion on your team (someone higher up in management who has a vested interest in making this work well) and, if applicable, people in other roles who are affected by the process. These people do not need to be full team members, but they should be enlisted to be available for consultation when needed.

In addition to listing the members of your working team, you need to identify other stakeholders. These people will not need to dedicate much time to the project, but you will need to consider them for information or approvals. These may include:

- Customers (internal or external) of the process output

- Suppliers of the process inputs (note that both suppliers and customers might be the owners of linking processes)

- Experts in any applicable standards or laws

- Anyone with considerable experience in how the process has been performed in the past or how it is performed in other companies

INVESTIGATING YOUR EXISTING CONDITIONS

Now that you've decided where you want to go, you need to figure out where you're starting from. Are you adding a new capability, or are you improving an existing one? The latter case can be further questioned: Are you improving an existing documented procedure, improving an undocumented (but generally recognized) process, or creating order out of chaos?

Once the challenge ahead of you has been defined, examine the resources that are currently either in place or able to be reallocated to this process, in terms of both people and infrastructure. For the human resources, this includes determining employees' skills and attitudes so that you know what training or hiring has to be done.

Working in a Green Field

On rare occasions, you are creating a new process where none has existed before. In this case, you need to investigate conditions under which the process will be running: What is the business climate? What are the needs of your customers (external or internal)? Who will be executing the process, and what is their level of expertise?

In some ways, it's a luxury to be in this position because you can take a totally fresh look at the situation without needing to account for past history, or you can take into account expectations of process users and customers that have been developed by past ways of working. On the other hand, this also means that you don't have the guidance of previous thought; it may not be immediately obvious who all the process's stakeholders are (or what their needs are).

Working in a Cultivated Field

More often you are working with an existing process, though there may not be a documented procedure. Sometimes there is more than one existing process or way of working in order to perform the same activities, and your job is to unify them.

Walk through the existing processes, literally if possible. If you can't directly observe, then interview the people who perform or are affected by the processes. Collect whatever data exists, and look for what is going right as well as what is going wrong. Map out the existing process, as a basis for discussion and as a tool to help you find existing issues. The same steps discussed in Chapter 7 to develop a new process map can also be used to map out an existing process.

Once you have your as-is process map, start looking for waste that can be eliminated. Two important concepts to consider are wait time and the hidden factory:

1. *Wait time* is time that occurs between activities on your process map, when nothing is being done. One example is waiting for approvals on a bid before the next task can happen. The idea of eliminating waste including wait time comes from Lean (discussed under the heading "Lean, Six Sigma, and Lean Six Sigma" in Chapter 3), which was developed for a manufacturing environment. It is not always a problem in business processes, but it is important often enough to be considered. If one of your goals is to reduce the time taken by the process, or if that would be a useful goal to add, then examine the as-is process(es) for wait time that can be eliminated. Typically, people try to make the activities themselves more efficient, but wait time usually dwarfs waste time within activities.

2. The *hidden factory* contains all those "unofficial" actions that people
    generally don't consider when mapping a process, but that take
    time and effort. Waiting for approval falls under the category of
    wait time, whereas going around the office trying to figure out who
    should approve the bid is a hidden factory activity. If you make
    these visible, you can figure out which of these activities can be
    eliminated or made more efficient (in this example, by a defined
    line of approvals). Tasks that no one else knows about may be per-
    formed by an individual; these need to be made visible partly to
    ensure that they really need to be done and partly so that others
    can follow the process.

REFINING YOUR GOALS

Now you have some data, whether it's quantitative or not. Examine
your findings, and look for opportunities for improvement. It may also
be helpful to benchmark similar processes or the same process in other
companies in order to get an idea of what improvements are possible.
When there are multiple existing ways of working, look for best practices that can be incorporated into the new procedure.

Determine whether your original goals are achievable, in light of
your new knowledge, and whether you can live with them, need to
tighten your scope, or can reasonably expand them or add to them
based on your findings. Consider the availability of resources in order
to determine what goals are realistic, and consider the needs of stakeholders (including suppliers, customers, management, and process users)
to determine what goals are required.

TAKING HUMAN NATURE
INTO CONSIDERATION

Now that you've figured out what you want to do, there are a few
things to think about before you start actually developing the process
into a standard documented procedure. You will find it much easier to

get people to follow your new procedure if you consider human nature from the beginning, both as you work on the procedure and as you talk to people about it.

Creating Procedures That People Want to Follow

The very best kind of procedure is one that is easier to follow than not to follow. A procedure can help people by showing them what to do so they don't have to figure it out each time, providing tooling to facilitate their work, and making expectations clearer for everyone involved.

> The very first business procedure I wrote was for my own use. I was a customer support engineer at a tiny software company, responsible for sending out new bug fixes to our customers. Each shipment involved sending a number of items (this was before Internet downloads were common) and getting a number of approvals. I sent out releases rarely enough that I didn't have all the steps memorized, so each time I had to figure out what I needed to include and who needed to sign off. To make it easier for myself and reduce the risk of errors, I created checklists and a script in Lotus Notes (I said this was a long time ago!) to walk me through the process and remind myself of everything that needed to be done. Later on, when someone else took over that responsibility, it was easy to hand it over because everything was documented.

This is what the idea of mistake-proofing (also known by the Japanese term *poka-yoke*) is about—constraining behavior so that procedures can be performed only in the right way. It's easiest to understand in procedures that require physical actions, and cars provide a couple of good examples. You can't start your car without pressing the brake pedal, for instance, so that your car doesn't immediately rocket down the street when you haven't checked ahead of you. At gas stations, diesel fuel nozzles are shaped differently from regular gas nozzles so that you can't put diesel into gasoline-powered cars. This is also a common technique in online processes: Amazon will not let me click on "Make Purchase" until

I've entered a valid credit card number. Think about whether your procedures can be mistake-proofed. It makes life easier for everyone if neither process users nor process owners need to worry about whether the procedure is being followed correctly.

The second-best procedure is one that may add a bit of work, but for which employees can easily see the benefit to themselves. For instance, if a customer service person at a call center is required to follow a script that includes informing all callers that calls may be recorded, she is protected from being charged with an illegal action (recording a call without permission) and also has evidence if the customer should later make untrue claims about the service provided.

The third-best procedure is one that may add a bit of work, but for which employees can easily see the benefit to the company. An example might be a case where a sales employee is required to get management approval to give customers discounts over a certain amount. This ensures that company policies are applied consistently, and also that the company's own financial needs are taken into account at the time a discount is given.

The worst procedure is one that goes against human nature—that introduces unneeded complexity, that adds extra work for no perceived gain, or that ignores logical and intuitive ways of working.

Other factors to consider are enhancing the visibility of the procedure and rewarding adherence to the procedure. For example:

- Is the procedure made visible such that others (including management) can easily tell if it's been properly followed? A good example here is clearly labeled tool storage boards, which make it obvious when tools are not returned or are stored incorrectly. Factories following Lean and Kanban (visual) methodologies use flags, signboards, and floor routing lines to make procedures visible. One way to do this in office procedures (at the low level of work instructions) is to require employees to record some value or comment for an action, rather than just check a box. For example, if the fuel level needs to be checked in a fleet car each morning, have the person write down the fuel quantity, rather than just check a box to say the fuel level was adequate.

- Do you have a "firefighting" culture, in which attention and rewards go to those who make heroic efforts and put in long hours to save a failing project? Or do managers prioritize and reward a process culture in which procedures are followed and work is done correctly the first time?

If none of these are true—that is, if the procedure adds extra effort for the employee, the employee can't see the benefit of following the procedure, it's not visible to others when the procedure is correctly followed, and management doesn't seem to care—you run the risk of passive resistance, in which employees simply don't follow the procedure. They may announce their intentions publicly or keep it quiet, but either way you have a real problem. This is especially so because having a procedure that people won't follow undermines the trust in your process system as a whole and increases the likelihood that other procedures won't be followed either.

Creating Procedures That
Don't Engender Resistance

Sometimes you encounter employees who just don't want to follow standard procedures, for whatever reason. They may dislike this specific procedure, or they may feel that standardization in general restricts their creativity. (I've encountered this reason mostly in areas that do demand some creativity, such as software development.) This is discussed in more detail in Chapter 13, but I want to talk about it now because the best way to deal with resistance is to build procedures that don't put people on the defensive in the first place. That means getting the procedure right, making it easy (or at least as easy as possible) to use, and having it for the right reason.

The first two of those—getting the procedure right and making it easy to use—are done by looking at the procedure from the point of view of its users, whether that's management for the high-level procedure that describes major functions of a department or the manufacturing tech who executes a work instruction. Try to consider the user's point of view while defining the process, and then ask him if you got it right. Better yet, include some users as part of the project team to develop the process.

Consider carefully not only whether a documented procedure is needed for a given process but also which parts of the process need to be standardized. For software development, for instance, standard formatting for headers, standard methods of describing inputs and outputs to a module of code, peer reviews, and standardized ways of logging time may all be useful, but when it comes to the creative part of the work, process experts, like managers, need to remove obstacles rather than create them.

IN-DEPTH EXAMPLE

Part I: Creating a Procedure for the "Process Improvement Process"

Let's walk through the steps of the process improvement for the example process introduced at the beginning of this chapter (in Figure 6-1). We will be working on developing a standard way to determine what needs to be improved for any given process and on capturing those improvements by creating a new process or revising an existing one. The first thing to do, in a real business environment, would be to decide which process to work on first, and I confess I made an arbitrary decision in order to have a clear example to use for this book. If I were doing this for a business purpose, I might want to spend more time deciding if this is the most important process to do first, or if it would be better to spend my team's time on something else. On the other hand, when you have a number of options of nearly equal value, sometimes it's better just to make an arbitrary decision and get started, rather than to get stuck in analysis paralysis. Also, in this case, the process improvement process is the foundation for all other process improvement; if you have lots of other processes that you need to improve, it might make sense to have a standard way to do so.

Let's assume we do not already have such a standard methodology, so we will be developing a new procedure. However, we know that process improvement has certainly been done before, so we want to investigate how it's been done, study the successes, and try to avoid the failures. Since we know that this is something that needs to happen in many companies, we should also take a look at available information on best practices in industry. (Pause for research . . . OK, let's pretend we've done that.)

Next, we define the goals of the process. Take a look at that high-level process map in Figure 6-1 again.

You can see that the next process in line, once we've determined and captured the new process, is the launch of the new process we've captured. What do we need to have in order to do that? In this case, we'd need a clear and complete procedure. We need to know who owns it, who will use it, what those users need to know in order to execute it, and what tooling or infrastructure they'll need. After the process is launched, we'll also need to be able to measure its operation, and then possibly come back and make improvements to it. That means we'll need to define the process to be transparent and measurable, so we can see what's happening and where it needs to improve.

To sum up, the goals of our process improvement process are: to create a clearly documented procedure with known ownership that meets the needs of its users and customers, whose performance can be measured. (The goal of our own project is to create an efficient, effective, and standardized way to produce such procedures.)

To determine the scope of the process, start with the trigger. In this case, we already have the higher-level parent process, so we can look and see what feeds into our process. From the previous processes, we've already seen a problem (or opportunity for improvement, which might include adding a new capability) and investigated the existing situation and the needs of the "customers." (I put "customers" in quotes as a reminder that they might be internal customers.) Thus, at this point, we know that we have a need for change, and we have some data on what is happening now and what the requirements are. Those are our triggers for figuring out and capturing a procedure. For the end point of our process, we can look back at our goals: This part of process improvement is done when we've captured a procedure, gotten it approved by the process owner and other needed approvers, aligned it with stakeholders, and published it so that it's ready to be launched.

We also need to consider what will be outside the scope of this process. For now, let's say that the process will govern only the improvement of documented procedures (or procedures that are to be documented), but not other items such as guidelines or policies. Another concern is what process levels will be included: Does it cover all levels from the top all the way down to the most detailed work instruction? It might be a good idea to leave out both the highest-level business model and the lowest-level work instructions: The former may need special approvals and more management backing for change, while this methodology might be overkill for something talking about the manufacture or replacement of a single part. We also need to consider which business areas are included: Will this be corporate-wide, or is it meant to apply only within a single department?

The answers to the question of scope will also determine the owner of the process. If this is meant to apply only to a single department, then the owner is whoever is mandating it for that department—either the department's manager or someone under her who is responsible for processes. If this process applies to more than one department, the owner is harder to define. In most cases it's not a great idea to have operational procedures owned by the quality department, but if that department is driving good process usage in the company, someone there might be the appropriate owner for this one. However, that will work only if there is buy-in from the management of affected departments or from the top management they report to. The scope of the process will also help determine who should be on the team to develop this procedure. If it needs to be workable for different groups, make sure they all have enough representation to make sure the end product is workable for them.

CHAPTER 7

Mapping Your Process

OK, YOU'RE DONE with all the preliminary stuff. Now it's time to get started drawing up a process! We begin by working from the outside in: looking at how the process interfaces with the outside world by figuring out what inputs are available to you, what inputs you will need that aren't currently available, and what outputs other people or processes require you to produce. After we've done that, we can begin to figure out what happens inside the process to convert those inputs into the required outputs.

UNDERSTANDING SIPOC
(THE "BLACK BOX" APPROACH)

A good way to start is with a *SIPOC*, which stands for Supplier-Input-Process-Output-Customer. This tool helps you figure out what your process needs to do, and what inputs are needed to do it, as well as who will use your outputs and who will supply your inputs.

We are going to use the "process improvement process" that we've been following in the In–Depth Example sections throughout the book to develop a sample SIPOC. Conveniently, we've already determined the goals and scope in Part I of that example.

Process

I've talked about creating a process from the outside in, but you create a SIPOC from the inside out, beginning with the process, as in Figure 7-1. Just draw it as a black box—at this point, you don't know what happens inside it.

FIGURE 7-1 SIPOC Process as a Black Box

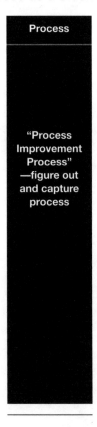

Outputs

Next, list the outputs you expect the process to produce, as demonstrated in Figure 7-2. Think about what success looks like for this process: What would you want to see to be sure the process was operating correctly? For a manufacturing process, this would include producing the final product within specifications, but it also might include the cost and time to produce it, any necessary documentation, calibration, and so forth. For a design process, the main output would be the design, but other outputs could include a log of the time to create the design, review records, approvals, make/buy decisions, component recommendations, and more.

FIGURE 7-2   SIPOC Process and Outputs

Process	Outputs
"Process Improvement Process" —figure out and capture process	Improved process is operational and its products meet specs
	Documented, approved procedure
	Trained users
	Necessary tooling developed and in place
	Defined KPIs, monitored and within spec
	Process records

If you look carefully at Figure 7-2 (which shows some typical outputs for process improvement), you see some redundancy in the list of outputs. One output is that whatever product is produced by the newly improved process meets its specifications, and another is the process KPIs. Some of those KPIs will certainly *be* those product specs, or a measurement of how well they're met (e.g., a KPI could be "99 percent of parts are measured within tolerance"). I listed the KPIs separately in this case because you may also have other KPIs, such as how long it takes to run the process (or intermediate steps of the process), which don't relate to the final outputs. Remember that the SIPOC is just a tool to help you figure out what a process should look like and to make sure it does everything it needs to do. Don't worry about getting it perfect; use the SIPOC to make sure you didn't miss anything in your process, but don't waste time obsessing over making it flawless.

Customers

List one or more customers for each output. As shown in Figure 7-3, these customers may be internal or external, but they should be the people who actually want and will use the output.

At this point, I began having to think hard about who the customers were for some outputs. I was tempted to list "quality department" as one customer of the documented procedure, and "auditors" as a customer of the records, but this is generally bad practice: Quality (including quality checks, such as audits) is a means to achieving satisfied customers, employees, and shareholders, rather than an end in itself. In this case, I thought more about who actually needs these outputs. For instance, users need a documented procedure so they can follow it; management needs process records, because if there's a problem, the manager who owns the process is responsible for getting it fixed, and records are one tool to figure out what's gone wrong. Records are also used during audits, but the audits in turn exist to inform managers of how well procedures are followed; to satisfy customers that there is a well-running, robust process system (needed to keep some customers,

FIGURE 7-3   SIPOC Process, Outputs, and Customers

Process	Outputs	Customers
	Improved process is operational and its products meet specs	External customer
"Process Improvement Process" —figure out and capture process	Documented, approved procedure	Process owner, process users, management
	Trained users	Line management
	Necessary tooling developed and in place	Users
	Defined KPIs, monitored and within spec	Management
	Process records	Management, users, some external customers

and thus a management concern); or to certify that a standard, such as ISO 9001 or AS9100, is being met, which again is all about staying in business.

Inputs

When you list the process inputs, include both inputs that will be changed by the process and resources that will be used but not changed (e.g., factory facilities). Remember to include intangibles like expertise, as shown in Figure 7-4.

FIGURE 7-4 SIPOC Inputs, Process, Outputs, and Customers

Inputs	Process	Outputs	Customers
Content expertise		Improved process is operational and its products meet specs	External customer
Process system	**"Process Improvement Process"**	Documented, approved procedure	Process owner, process users, management
Process expertise	**—figure out and capture process**	Trained users	Line management
Information on customer needs		Necessary tooling developed and in place	Users
Existing process, if applicable		Defined KPIs, monitored and within spec	Management
		Process records	Management, users, some external customers

When you're working on more concrete processes, you have more concrete inputs. These might include raw materials, factory or lab facilities and equipment, data, request forms, market research, a safety code, partially completed parts, and so forth. However, even in these cases, you still have intangible inputs, such as special knowledge or skills. It's a good idea to list these so that you can verify that you have a supplier for them.

Suppliers

Finally, list the supplier for each input, as shown in Figure 7-5. In this case, because I'm devising a generic process for process improvement that would work for any company, it's difficult to say who the suppliers of inputs are because they vary so much. Within a specific corporation, it would be more obvious who owned the process system or an existing process, for instance. For a more concrete process, it should be even easier to figure out who supplies the raw materials, the forms, the rules, the policies, and any other inputs.

FIGURE 7-5 SIPOC Suppliers, Inputs, Process, Outputs, and Customers

Suppliers	Inputs	Process	Outputs	Customers
Process owner, users, and other experts in content area	Content expertise		Improved process is operational and its products meet specs	External customer
Process system owner	Process system	**"Process Improvement Process" —figure out and capture process**	Documented, approved procedure	Process owner, process users, management
Process expert	Process expertise		Trained users	Line management
Customers, Marketing, Customer service	Information on customer needs		Necessary tooling developed and in place	Users
Process owner	Existing process, if applicable		Defined KPIs, monitored and within spec	Management
			Process records	Management, users, some external customers

Examine the completed SIPOC to see if there are any obvious issues. If you have an output and haven't been able to name any customers for it, consider if maybe that output is not needed. If that's the case, you may be able to eliminate this process, or a part of it. Again, if you have an input without suppliers, you need to ask yourself some questions. If this input is really needed in order to perform the process, then you're going to have to find someone who can supply it. Also, if there are any new inputs or changes to existing inputs, you will need to negotiate this with the suppliers to make sure they can provide what is needed, at the right time, and in the needed quantity.

Now you have a good idea of where the process begins and ends, and you are ready to gain some visibility into that black box.

DEVELOPING A PROCESS MAP

You have determined the goals of your process, defined its scope and boundaries, and identified its stakeholders. Now you're ready to begin creating a procedure. The heart of the procedure is the process map, and that should be where you start. Gather your key stakeholders and sit down to agree on what tasks need to be done to fill in that black box from the SIPOC to get you from input to output.

Grab your team and your sticky notes, book a conference room for a few hours (your team will really appreciate it if you order in lunch!), and brainstorm the tasks in your process and how they relate to each other.

Essentially, a process map is a glorified flowchart (though it can include additional information), and process maps generally use standard flowchart symbols, like those in Figure 7-6. The rectangle for a process step, the diamond for a decision point, and the oblong for a terminator are the most commonly used symbols; I've also added shapes to show process triggers and linkages where I needed them. You can use other symbols if you need to, either standard ones or your own. Just be sure to add a legend defining your symbols if they may be unclear to your reading audience.

FIGURE 7-6 Process Map Symbols

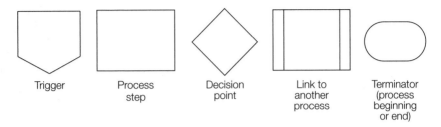

Trigger   Process   Decision   Link to   Terminator
           step   point   another   (process
                                  process   beginning
                                             or end)

In addition, some process maps may show the roles of the people who perform each step (either with swim lanes, discussed later in this chapter, or icons), wait time, inputs and outputs from each step, or other information. Whatever information you decide to include, be careful to ensure that your process maps are easily readable by their target audience. I've seen some that require intense study or lengthy text to be understood, which rather defeats the purpose of depicting the process graphically.

Now we're ready to begin filling in the black box in the middle of that SIPOC with our process steps. When creating a process map, work from the outside in, which means you start at the beginning and end of your process. You already know how the process begins, with the process trigger. Write it down. Next, figure out where the process ends. You've already determined the process goals. How do you know when they've been reached? The SIPOC can help with this: You're done when all of the outputs have been produced, at a quality level that meets the needs of the customer for each output. (If producing those outputs does not satisfy the process goals, then you have a mismatch somewhere—either you have missing outputs or your goals are not feasible and need to be reworked.) When you figure that out, that's your end point. For instance, a high-level manufacturing process, one that produces a finished product, might end when the product is tested and meets specifications. A lower-level child subprocess might end when a certain feature has been machined into a component of that product and is measured to be within spec.

Next look at the SIPOC: You have one set of inputs, and you need to produce a different set of outputs. How do you get there from here? What intermediate outputs are needed in order to create the final process outputs, and what tasks must be done to produce them?

Brainstorming Process Tasks and Flow

In most cases, it's best to get your team together to create the process flow. There may be a few exceptions. For a simple work instruction where you thoroughly understand what needs to be done, for example, it might make more sense to just draw it out yourself and then get others to review it. Usually, though, it's best to bring the group together to make sure that the important perspectives are represented and nothing is overlooked. Good facilitation skills are essential here. (See Chapter 12 for more information on facilitating.)

If you have a fairly inexperienced group or a shy one that is reluctant to speak up, it is best to draft a first version of a flowchart yourself and take it in to the group meeting to spur discussion and critique. Don't worry if you don't know the process well; it doesn't actually matter if you get it completely wrong in this initial draft. In my experience, when people are not sure where to start, they often do better if they have a "straw man" target to throw darts at. They will criticize your first draft and quite possibly end up with something completely different. Also, the initial draft at least gives your team an idea of what a process map should look like: what symbols you are using, what level of detail you expect to see, and so forth. You might want to display the initial draft to the team either by projecting an editable version for all to see, so that you can move things around and change wording as the discussion evolves, or by placing sticky notes on a whiteboard, one note for each process step, with arrows to show the flow between them. That way, the group members themselves can redraw arrows on the board, move steps around, add or subtract process steps, or replace badly worded tasks with new ones.

Another way is for you, as facilitator, to lead a group discussion on each step. Begin with the previously agreed-upon trigger or starting point for the process, and ask what happens next, what happens after that, and so forth. Once you've agreed on what process steps are needed in the procedure, you need to determine the order and how you move from one to another. Pay particular attention to what happens when there is a point where things can go in different directions depending on the outcome of a given step, and make sure you capture all outcomes. You can show these as a loop, in a higher-level process map such as in Figure 7-7, or make the decision point clear, such as in Figure 7-8. In general, the more detailed (that is, the lower the level) your procedure is, the more important it becomes to show decisions explicitly.

FIGURE 7-7   A Process Loop

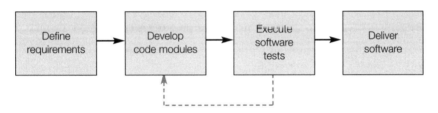

FIGURE 7-8   A Process Decision Point

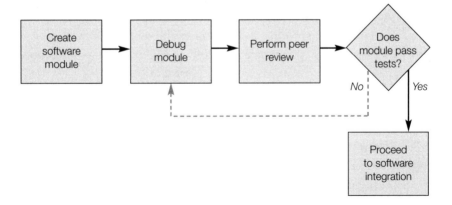

If you have a knowledgeable and opinionated group with a variety of perspectives on the process, and especially if you are working on a new process whose flow is not yet well understood, you might want to try a more creative brainstorming approach, and you might not need to create a straw man draft before the meeting. In this case, you can use the sticky notes to help your stakeholders brainstorm a process flow from scratch. Give each person a marker and a pile of sticky notes, allow the team fifteen minutes or so to write down each task, then group similar items, and agree on wording for each process step. (There are lots of different ways to do this, of course. I just like using sticky notes because they provide a visual diagram that's easy for everyone to understand and because they can be moved around easily as the group consensus develops.)

Once your group has agreed on the basic process flow, document it in a more permanent and readable form, using something like PowerPoint or Microsoft Visio to draw the process map. It can be helpful to bring a digital camera or a phone with a good camera to the process map meeting, so that you can take a picture of the agreed-upon flow, and use that as a reference to draw it up later. Otherwise, just make a quick copy on paper and then draw it up properly afterward. Bring this cleaned-up version to the next group meeting to make sure that everyone agrees that you've correctly captured what was decided, as well as to see if there are any further changes or clarifications to be made.

Now let's compare two sample process maps. Both of these are drawn in PowerPoint: Figure 2-4 (found in the section "Developing a Process Hierarchy" in Chapter 2) is a high-level toy design process, and Figure 7-9, shown here, is a low-level travel request process.

You can immediately see some differences between the two process maps. The first one, in Figure 2-4, is a high-level map. Several of the steps within it are complete processes that can be expanded into process maps of their own. At this level, we don't go into detail. There are three verification/validation stages (verify that design satisfies requirements; verify proto meets requirements; have user group test prototype), and it's clear that there will be some looping, because the design will need to be adapted whenever issues are found. But at this level, we

FIGURE 7-9   Travel Request Process Map

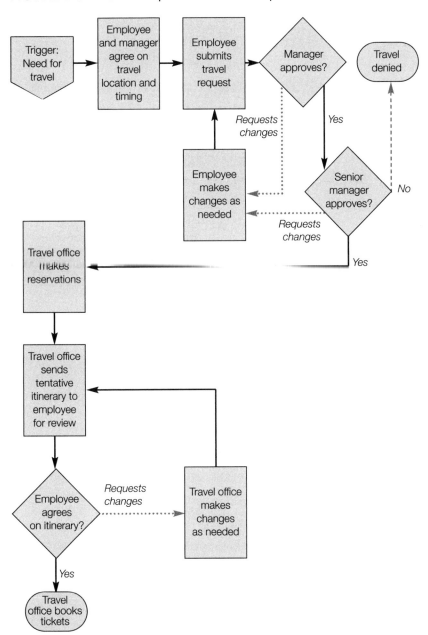

don't really need to show exactly what decisions have to be made to enter each of those loops; those can be explained in the lower-level procedures.

On the other hand, the travel request process map in Figure 7-9 is low-level and detailed, with decision points indicated. This process map might not need any subprocesses at all (except maybe a work instruction for how to book travel), and each step is performed by one individual, except for when the employee and her manager agree together on the need for travel. Another difference between the two process maps is that Figure 7-9 uses flowchart symbols for the starting trigger, the decision points, and the two possible end points of the process, whereas Figure 2-4 doesn't really show decisions to be made and is less clear about the start and end point of the process. In that respect, Figure 7-9 is clearer, but in the other case, it's OK for decisions, triggers, and actions to be clarified in the subprocesses.

Establishing Roles and Responsibilities Within the Process

Once your team agrees on the process steps, determine who will perform each action. This can be an individual, a team, or, at the highest level, even a department. (I refer to them as people here; just bear in mind that for larger tasks it might be a team or group.) Because people move around within an organization, it is better to list these by role (e.g., Manufacturing Product Cell Lead) than by name.

You can show who performs each step by using color-coding or swim lanes (discussed in detail later). However, to provide a fuller understanding, it is common to include a *RACI matrix* in a procedure. This assigns up to four roles to each process step, showing who is responsible for each role. Note, again, that the person or persons in each role should be identified by title, not by name, to allow for change within the organization. The four roles are:

1. **R:** person who is *responsible*—does the work, or controls the work-hours of the people who do the work

2. **A**: person who is *accountable*—ensures that the work gets done and takes action if not

3. **C**: person who is *contributing*—helps get the work done

4. **I**: person who is *informed*—is notified when work is done for each action

The RACI matrix can be extremely useful in higher-level procedures as it gives you a path of escalation in case something goes wrong, via the accountable person; makes sure stakeholders are kept involved in the contributing role; and lets process users know who needs to be kept informed of the process's execution.

Use your judgment about when to include a RACI matrix. It would probably be overkill in a work instruction; you don't want to have to think about who is accountable or who should be contributing or informed every time you turn a knob, replace a filter, or fill out a purchase request. However, it might be useful to know who is accountable for making sure employee appraisals get done or who should be asked to contribute when new training materials are developed.

You can have any number of people listed in the C and I roles, contributing to and being informed of process decisions and milestones, but it's important to have only one person in the A role. This is the individual who makes decisions when something goes wrong with the process, and it's necessary to have a clear path of escalation.

There are conflicting opinions on whether you can have more than one person in the R role. Some people say that it's crucial to have only one center of responsibility for performing each task, but in practice, it can sometimes be difficult. (Actually, everyone I've discussed this with agrees that it's better to have one person take responsibility; the disagreement is only on whether it's ever allowable to have more than one.) You might have different people performing tasks in different circumstances or in different regions. For instance, looking at the travel request process map in Figure 7-9, in a small office people might be responsible for booking their own flights, whereas in larger offices that function might be handled by a dedicated travel team. You can generally resolve this by either describing who handles the role under which circumstances (if there is a travel office, then it books plane tickets; otherwise, the employee is responsible for booking his or her own) or by describing the role in terms of the responsibility, and including explanation (plane tickets are booked by the travel coordinator, with a statement that the coordinator might either be the employee or a dedicated person in a travel office).

If your group is anything like the ones I've worked with, discussions about the roles and responsibilities within a process can sometimes get bogged down in minutiae and become much too long, breeding conflicts and wasting people's time with details that won't really make much difference in the long run. Here are a few suggestions to minimize those discussions and make them both effective and efficient:

- *Define your rules beforehand.* Will you allow more than one person in the R role? How about the A role? (This is not recommended.) Must the A role be the hierarchical supervisor of the R role, or can it be someone with functional responsibilities that cross lines of the org chart? What recourse do contributors have if their contribution is changed or rejected?

- *Determine whether a full RACI table is required.* You can choose *not* to use a RACI matrix unless it's a company standard—or, maybe, you can use it only for your highest-level processes and not for the others. Do you really need to know who has authority for every action in the process map, or is it enough to have a defined escalation path for the process overall, in case it is not going as planned? Especially in lower-level/higher-detail procedures, the R role may be all you need to know. Remember to include only the level of detail that is actually useful in the operations of your company.

- *Set time limits.* If the team can't agree on a role in five minutes of discussion, cut it short, set that issue aside, and go on to the next process step. Often, further discussion helps to clarify the team's thinking, so that you can come back to a difficult issue and find that it has been stripped of its thorns. (This approach also works for many other arguments you might have in the course of creating or revising a procedure.)

IN-DEPTH EXAMPLE

Part II: Developing a Process Map for the "Process Improvement Process"

Let's revisit the process improvement example that we've been discussing. We know how our process fits into its higher-level parent process (see Figure 6-1 near the beginning of Chapter 6), and earlier in this chapter we developed a SIPOC. Now it's time to walk through the development of a process map.

We also know a few other things about the process:

Goal: The goal is to create a clearly documented procedure, with known ownership and that meets the needs of its users and customers, whose performance can be measured.

Scope: All improvements of standardized processes across the company will be governed by this procedure. The trigger is that we have decided to change and have acquired data about the current situation and customer needs. The process improvement process ends when we have captured a procedure, gotten it approved by the process owner (and other needed approvers), aligned it with its stakeholders, and published it so that it's ready to be launched.

Owner and project team: In this case, the owner is the head of the quality department, with the backing of upper management. The team is led by a delegate from within the quality department and includes a business process analyst, who can provide process expertise plus facilitation skills, as well as a representative from each major department that will use this procedure.

(Continued on next page)

OK. So we know where we have started and where we want to end. Now we just have to fill in the middle, as shown in Figure 7-10.

FIGURE 7-10   Beginning to Figure Out the "Process Improvement Process"

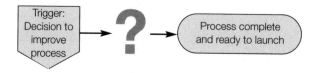

Clearly it's time to start brainstorming. Luckily, we have two things: (1) data on the current situation and the customer's requirements for the procedure we want to improve, and (2) this whole chapter (which will tell us how to do it). By the time we've reached this point in the parent process, we know which process we're improving and that we are improving it somehow, not just documenting it. So the first thing to do is to determine the process goals, based on the customer's needs, and the next thing to do is to figure out the scope and boundaries of the process. (See Figure 7-11.)

FIGURE 7-11   The Next Step in Figuring Out the "Process Improvement Process"

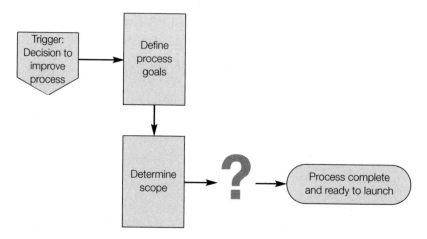

We can keep going in this way, alternately asking ourselves three questions:

1. What happens next?

2. Is that activity really needed?

3. How can we make this process easier to use?

And adding in a fourth now and then:

4. Have we missed anything?

Eventually, after much discussion and several rounds of questions, we end up with something like Figure 7-12. It's still not perfect; this is only a first draft. The next step will be to review it with the team, to walk through the process (literally or metaphorically) until the team is agreed that it's right, and then to go on and document the rest of the procedure.

FIGURE 7-12   First Draft of the Process Map for the "Process Improvement Process"

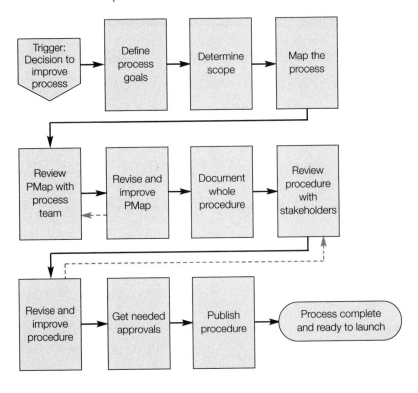

PRESENTING SOME VARIATIONS
ON PROCESS MAPS

As with most things related to business processes, there's more than one good way to draw a process map. Here are some variations you may find useful.

Swim Lanes

You may choose to use *swim lanes*, to show graphically who is responsible for each process step. A swim lane is a column for each involved role or department, into which the steps performed by that role are placed. Figure 7-13 shows the travel request process map from Figure 7-9 redrawn to use swim lanes.

As you can see, the process steps have had to be rearranged in order to fit within the swim lanes. This can be an advantage or a drawback for clarity. You don't have to state who performs which step (e.g., "Manager approves?" and "Senior manager approves?" in Figure 7-9); these can just be written as "Approves?" here. However, sometimes it can be difficult to arrange the process steps in a logical way within the constraints of the swim lanes.

Six Sigma Style

It's useful to have a variety of tools in your toolbox, just so that you have the right one when you need it. The Six Sigma variant of process mapping may or may not be useful to you, but if you know how to do it, then you have the choice. Most people draw process maps as a simple flowchart, but because Six Sigma, as discussed in Chapter 3, is about minimizing variation (and thus producing outputs of consistent quality), its version of process mapping goes a bit further.

Here's how you create this type of process map. Once you've determined what steps are in your process and how they're linked, take a good look at each one, and write down the inputs and outputs for that specific step (not for the process as a whole). Then, next to each input, write C if it is *controllable,* N if it is *not controllable,* SOP if it is a *standard operating process,* and X if it is *critical* to the whole process's output.

FIGURE 7-13 Travel Request Process Map with Swim Lanes

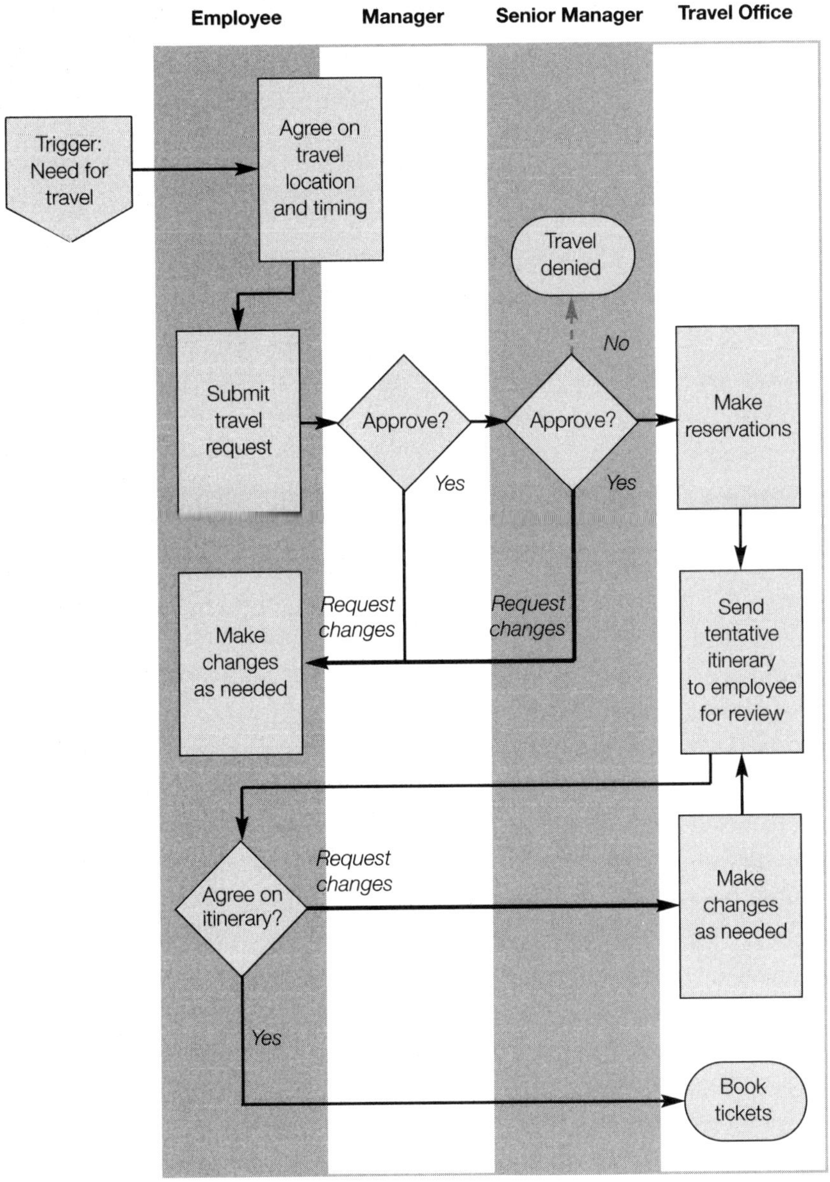

This allows you to do two things:

1. You can examine the process step outputs to see if all of them are used, either within the process or by internal/external customers. If an output is not used, consider whether the step that produced it is waste that could be eliminated.

2. You can determine which inputs need to be controlled, and then you can decide how to control them, in order to guarantee quality and minimize variation in your process's output.

This style of process map works best when you have a number of quantitative inputs for at least several of the steps. It can be difficult, but not impossible, to do this for a more qualitative process, and it can be useful in opening up discussion of what inputs are really essential and which ones can be changed if needed. An example of this type of process map is shown in Figure 7-14.

Let's look more closely at a couple of the process steps in this example, in order to understand the classification of their inputs. The task "Determine time and facilities needed for training" has three inputs (tooling needed to follow process; amount of information to convey; number of trainees). The tooling required to execute the process will be needed for training, if the training is hands-on; it is controllable (C) because it's possible to develop a training method that doesn't have to be hands-on. The number of trainees is probably not something that can be changed, since it depends on how many people will need to follow the process and will need training to do so, and the amount of information to convey will depend on the knowledge level of the trainees and the complexity of the process. The task "Decide on timing and location of training" has two inputs (availability of facilities; availability of trainers/trainees), both critical (X). You can have the training only at a time when training facilities and people (both trainers and trainees) are available. Note that this critical input may also be controllable: If the priority of the training is high enough, schedules can be freed up.

FIGURE 7-14 Training Planning Process Map in Six Sigma Style

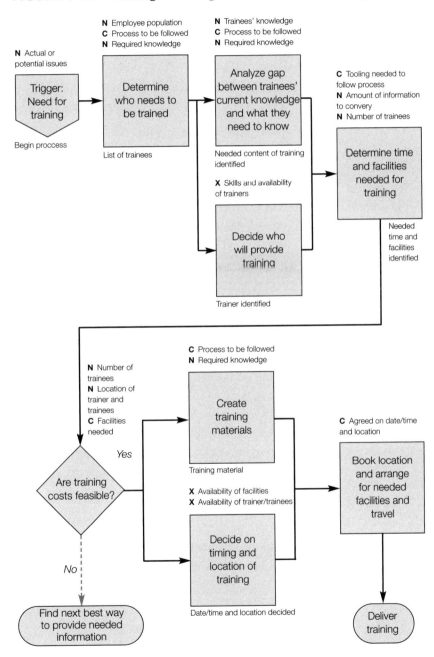

Note that in this example, the process on which employees are to be trained is listed as C, controllable. That's because if you simplify the process, less training should be required. Availability of people and facilities are also shown as controllable, because usually this is a matter of priority. As already stated, if the priority is high enough, schedules can be freed up.

Value Stream Mapping

Value Stream Maps (VSMs) are a Lean tool, invented for use in improving manufacturing processes. Like most Lean tools, they have come to be used in other areas as well. VSMs generally start with a relatively simple process map, showing either the main steps of a process at a high level or the specifics of a simple lower-level process, generally in a linear flow. For each step, they show data about the flow of materials and information, such as elapsed time for that step and information about the material and work in process at that step, as well as wait time between process steps.

Figure 7-15 shows a portion of a typical hiring process. In this case, the hiring manager is really the customer, the job applicants are the suppliers (of their own skills and work), and the human resources department controls the timing of the process. You can see the information flow among the three sets of people involved, and there is room within each process step's box to show some metrics for that step. This example shows the utility of VSMs in pointing out a common misunderstanding among people who set out to streamline processes. Often, these improvers try to eliminate waste within the steps of the process, but as you can see here, the time actually needed to execute each process step is dwarfed by the idle time (that is, idle from the point of view of the process) between the steps.

For more detail, as well as some variant types of VSMs, I recommend *The Lean Six Sigma Guide to Doing More with Less* by Mark O. George. You can also find articles on the use of VSMs on the iSixSigma website, http://www.isixsigma.com.

FIGURE 7-15   Partial Value Stream Map for a Hiring Process

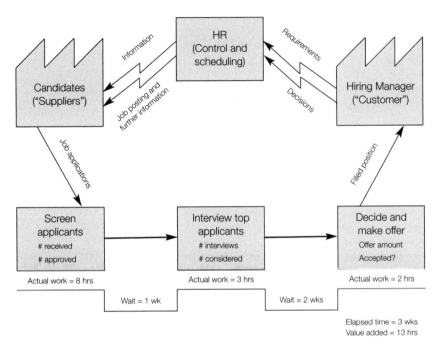

INCORPORATING PROCESS MAPS
WITH WORK INSTRUCTIONS (OR NOT)

A process map can occasionally add clarity to a work instruction. A work instruction is the lowest level of procedure; since a work instruction gives detailed step-by-step instructions for following a process, it is sometimes helpful to include a picture of each step. If this adds clarity to the work instruction, then go ahead and incorporate a process map; but if it won't, then don't, because it only adds unnecessary length.

For example, a work instruction for putting gas in a car could read:

- *Step 1:* Monitor fuel gauge on dashboard; initiate refueling process whenever fuel level falls below a quarter of a tank according to the gauge.

- *Step 2:* Examine car and determine whether access to fuel tank is on driver's side or passenger's side.

- *Step 3:* Pull up to fuel pump with appropriate side (the one with the fuel cap) facing pump. Place car in "Park" and turn off engine.

- *Step 4:* Enter credit card in appropriate slot on fuel pump, then withdraw card. When indicator screen signals that the pump is ready, open fuel tank (this may require a key or a latch inside the car, or simply pressing on one side of the fuel flap), and unscrew fuel cap.

- *Step 5:* Take nozzle from side of fuel pump, ensuring that you have selected a gas hose and not a diesel hose, and place nozzle in fuel tank.

 . . . And so on.

This work instruction could include a picture of a fuel gauge in Step 1, a gearshift placed in "Park" for Step 3, a credit card being inserted in the credit-card slot of a fuel pump in Step 4, a nozzle being inserted in a fuel tank for Step 5, and so forth. It would also be a useful safety precaution to provide a visual example of the differences between gas and diesel nozzles.

If there are multiple steps in a work instruction, and if the process can fork depending on conditions or results of previous steps, a process map does add clarity. For instance, in the car-fueling example, you could have a decision point that says, "Does the car take diesel fuel?" If the answer is "yes," then you would fork to a process step to choose a gas station and pump that provide diesel; if not, then you would proceed with the steps as shown above.

In other words, follow *Rule C* and *Rule M:* Customize work instructions to your needs, and avoid padding them with information that does not add value.

REEVALUATING AND IMPROVING THE PROCESS

Once you've created the first draft of your process map, it's a good idea to step back and take another look at what you have to make sure you haven't left anything out or misstated anything. The process map is not only a way to communicate the workings of a procedure to other people. It also allows you to see your process in a new way. This is a good time to see where you can make the process more effective or efficient (assuming you are creating or improving a process, rather than simply documenting one that already exists). Don't do this immediately after creating the process map; instead, come back to it on another day so you can look at it with fresh eyes. Often, you are limited by the availability of your project team. If it's not possible to schedule another team meeting, you can ask the team members to review it individually. If you have to do it that way, it might be a good idea to create a checklist, based on this section, to give people an idea of what they should be looking for.

Confirming Inputs and Outputs

There are several things to look for here. Check the process map against the SIPOC, and verify the following:

- Have you actually captured all the steps required to get from input to output?

- Are all inputs from the process used, and are all necessary outputs created?

- While creating the process, were additional inputs and outputs identified? (If so, you need to update the SIPOC.)

- Check the inputs and outputs of every step: Are all inputs available? Are all outputs actually used?

- Thinking of all the data needed in the process, is it all accounted for? Should some of this data have been listed as inputs or outputs?

- What records will need to be kept? Confirm that each critical record is included as an output within the process. (At this point, just worry about the most important ones; the records section can be more fully filled in later.)

Establishing Loops and Branches

Notice whether your process includes any loops—for instance, where a draft will be created, reviewed, and amended until it passes a review or test. If your process provides a single path through all tasks, with no looping back and no divisions to show paths through tasks that can be performed in parallel, you should be suspicious of the process map's accuracy. Check to see if one of the following is true:

1. The process map is a greatly simplified model at the very highest level of abstraction, as with Figures 2-3 or 6-1. This is OK; it is meant to show how top-level processes fit together, but not how to step through a single process.

2. The process map is at the very lowest level, a detailed work instruction for a simple task. This is also OK, though you may want to consider if a simple checklist or diagram would be enough information.

3. The process map is idealized and assumes that every deliverable is going to be perfect the first time through. In that case, you may need to push your stakeholders a bit to think about what's likely to happen in a real situation.

4. The process map is wrong: Some steps have not been documented. The Lean methodology discusses the concept of the "hidden factory," in which an idealized process map conceals a flurry of activity that has to happen for the process to succeed, but that is not shown on the map. It's rather like watching a swan glide serenely over a pond without seeing the churning feet below that propel it through the water.

Checking the People and the Transitions Between Them

As before, when I say "people," this may also include teams or departments—any entity that is responsible for performing a process step. Think of all the people who are currently involved in the process, or who should be involved in a new process, and see if their contributions are included. Bear in mind that not all current steps need to be included; you may decide that some are wasteful and should be omitted. Also, consider all the stakeholders: Are all their needs met by the process you've just drawn up?

Look also at the tasks assigned to each person involved. One way to reduce wait time is to make sure that the process steps don't bounce back and forth between people more than necessary. For example, if the first step is assigned to Tom, the second to Jun, the third to Tom again, the fourth to Yvonne, and the fifth to Jun, is it possible for you to streamline the procedure so that Tom and Jun can each complete all their tasks at one time, without needing to wait for each other?

Searching Out and Eliminating Waste and Delay

Ask these questions, and add your own:

- Are there process steps that don't contribute in any way to the final outputs or the efficiency of the process? If so, kill them off.

- Are there likely to be long delays between the process steps? If so, is there a way to safeguard against these delays? Often these delays dwarf inefficiencies in the actual process steps. If you're trying to reduce the time it takes to execute a process, eliminating delays between steps is a good place to start.

- Can you simplify the path through the process?

- Think about dependencies of process steps—that is, which ones require inputs produced by previous steps, or which ones make use of the same people, tools, or other resources. Do you show process steps in series that could be performed in parallel?

- What happens if process steps do not happen correctly? If you're improving an existing process, you may find that there are common ways to deal with these problems that have not been documented. If it's a new process, you will need to build in these controls.

- Remember the concept of the hidden factory. Are people going to have to do behind-the-scenes work that you haven't shown in order to accomplish the steps you have shown? Is there likely to be wait time between the process steps, and if so, is it possible to eliminate it?

Performing a Real-World Check

This is a good time to walk through the final process and make sure it makes sense. When this step is forgotten, you can end up with something that looks great on paper but doesn't make sense to the people who will actually follow the procedure. If possible, do this walk-through literally and physically by executing the process in real life and seeing if it works. If that's not possible, walk through it in your imagination, preferably together with one or more of the people who will execute the process.

IN-DEPTH EXAMPLE

Part III: Revising the Process Map for the "Process Improvement Process"

To bring our ongoing process improvement example up to date, I took the first draft of the process map created in the previous installment of our In-Depth Example (Figure 7-12) and reviewed it against the ideas we've talked about in this chapter. As you can see in the second draft, in Figure 7-16, a few things were indeed missing: Process ownership was never explicitly determined, and the SIPOC was never mentioned. (It's part of mapping the process and could thus have been omitted, but in some cases it might be a good thing to mention the SIPOC specifically, particularly if it's part of a change you're making in how process improvement works at your company.) I also added a link to the launch-planning process, using a rectangle with two lines on either side to show that it's a link to a process defined elsewhere.

FIGURE 7-16   Second Draft of the Process Map for the
                 "Process Improvement Process"

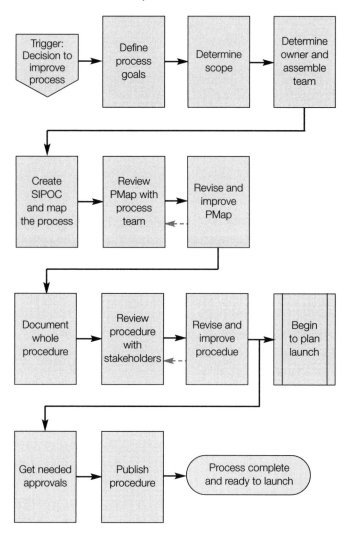

CHAPTER 8

Documenting the Rest of Your Procedure

THE PROCESS MAP is the heart of your procedure. Now that you've created a draft, you can analyze the function of that heart and begin to build the whole body of the procedure around it.

At this point, you know enough about the process to begin understanding what it will look like when it's operating in the real world, so you can determine what infrastructure is needed to allow the process to function and what key process indicators are needed to measure its operation. You may find it necessary to create a draft first, with some sections left blank, to help your process improvement team visualize the process in more detail. If possible, though, it's more efficient to make these decisions now. You may find that you need to make changes once the procedure is fleshed out in more detail, but the advantage to making these decisions first is that the procedure can be written from the start with these considerations known. If you add them only after the first draft, that creates another review and revision cycle, and the changes to infrastructure and KPIs may force changes to other parts of the procedure.

DETERMINING INFRASTRUCTURE NEEDS

Consider what infrastructure must be in place before the new process can take effect. Will you need new tooling, parts, or test fixtures? Will you need to add facilities or make changes to existing ones? What training materials need to be developed? Do you need to hire any new people or move existing ones around? Will you need to have process experts in place at the beginning, or even on an ongoing basis, in order to provide guidance to others using the procedure? These items are really all part of planning your launch, but this is the time to consider them so that you don't have long delays between completing your procedure document and beginning to use it.

Consider also whether your procedure can stand on its own or whether any other procedures need to be changed or created before this one can function.

DEFINING KEY PROCESS INDICATORS

Key Process Indicators (KPIs) are metrics that can be monitored. KPIs let you know whether the process is being followed and whether it's working as desired. You may want to document them within the procedure, or you may need to if KPIs are included in your procedure template. The disadvantage to documenting them is that you will then need to revise your procedure whenever you want to change your KPIs. To maintain flexibility, I recommend not including your KPI target values inside the procedure, because these almost certainly will change. To make your procedure more flexible, you may choose to include language like "This procedure will be instrumented with KPIs measuring cycle time and adherence to cost/schedule estimates" (or whatever general item you will be measuring). Then you can change the specific definition of your KPIs as needed.

Even if specific KPIs will not be documented within the procedure, you definitely need to know at least your most critical KPIs by the time you're ready to implement your changes, so start thinking about them now. One way to consider KPIs is to think about what success looks like—that is, what is happening when your process is running correctly? How would that be different if it's not working well? How can this vision of success be converted into quantifiable, objective data? (See Chapter 11 for more detailed discussion of how to select KPIs.)

MANAGING RISK

Think about what can go wrong with the process and what controls you have to either make sure those things don't happen or to make sure they don't hurt much if they do (that is, to prevent or mitigate the risk). You can use your process map to spark ideas for this: Look at each step, and try to think about what risks it has. You may decide that some risks aren't worth planning for because it costs more resources (people, time, money) to prevent or minimize them than it does just to deal with whatever may happen. Other risks—such as those that are more likely to happen or that have the potential to cause more harm—are worth planning for.

You can handle risks in different ways. In some cases, you may need to change the procedure itself to avoid major problems that are likely to crop up otherwise. In other cases, it's enough to define an *escalation path* so that it's clear where problems should be reported and who's responsible for fixing them. (An escalation path defines increasing levels of responsibility for fixing a problem. For example, if the process is not working well, the person monitoring it should report the issue to the process owner. If the owner is not able to fix the problem with available resources, he then reports it to the next level of management, and so on up the chain.)

CREATING A FIRST DRAFT OF THE PROCEDURE

This is where the ink hits the paper, or at least where the electrons hit the ... um, other electrons. Once your team has determined the process scope and goals and agreed on the basic process flow, it's time to create the procedure. You should have already defined a procedure template as part of your process system; if not, determine what information you want to include in your procedure. (You may find the discussion "Creating Templates for Standard Procedures" in Chapter 3 helpful.)

Take your process goals, scope, inputs, outputs, process map, decisions on who performs each action, and whatever else you know about the process, and use this information to fill in your procedure template. (If your company doesn't have a procedure template, you can use the one in the Appendix as a starting point, customizing it to your needs.) Try to use language that is as clear and simple as possible—remember, you may be an expert on the process, but your readers aren't. The whole point of a procedure is to explain how a process works.

One of the tips given earlier for work instructions applies to higher-level procedures as well: Include images and diagrams whenever they make the procedure clearer, and avoid including any information that does not add value.

It is best to have a single person do the actual writing, but this person needs to consult other members of the process team. Try to include the entire team. This may, after all, be the first time anyone has looked at all the process information together, and it often happens that the parts affect one another. For instance, while documenting the process map, you may realize that the team has included some items that are out of scope, or that one person has been given several tasks that have to be performed at the same time. Depending on the relationship among the team members, their availability, their physical proximity, and your company culture, it may be better to schedule regular reviews or just have a lot of informal discussions. Make sure that all team members are notified and given a chance to discuss any changes to the process that are made necessary by realizations that come up while documenting the procedure.

IN-DEPTH EXAMPLE

Part IV: Completing the Procedure for the "Process Improvement Process"

In the last installment of this In-Depth Example (at the end of Chapter 7), we created a process map, so the next step—after reviewing and revising it with the team—is to fill in the rest of the procedure. I'm not going to include an entire procedure here, but I discuss some of the other points to be considered in completing the process improvement procedure.

Infrastructure

An environment needs to be in place, providing a library where you can check in procedures, a way to maintain the correct versions, and a location (usually an intranet page) to publish procedures so that they are available to all users. If the system is not already in place, it needs to be developed and installed. (See Chapter 3 for a detailed discussion of the requirements for such systems.)

Process owners need to be defined for all procedures, and these individuals need to be made aware of their responsibilities. Users need to be told to always reference the latest version of any procedure; after all, you don't want people working from a hard copy, printed at some unknown time in the past, that might be several versions out of date.

KPIs

KPIs for our process improvement procedure might include the ratio of the number of procedures published to the number identified, the percentage of procedures published whose own KPIs are actively being monitored by management, the percentage of procedure-related KPIs that are achieving their targets, the number of process-related audit findings currently open, and so forth. (These are meant to be possible considerations, not a hard-and-fast list to be followed for any process improvement procedure.)

(Continued on next page)

Risk Management

Think about what can go wrong with process improvement and how to avoid those risks or minimize their impact. It's possible that process improvement projects are initiated that are not really justified. One way to deal with this risk is to set up a mechanism (such as a board that meets quarterly) to decide which projects to do.

A list of risks and plans to mitigate them could be incorporated in the procedure for our example process.

DEFINING TERMS

As you write your procedure, try to make your language as unambiguous as possible. Be especially careful about any words that have particular meanings in your field but have different meanings in general usage; this is common in medical and other technical fields. Examples are the definitions for "process" and "procedure" given at the start of this book.

Another place to be careful is the use of verbs such as "shall," "will," and "may." Some industries and organizations (including NASA) use the following standard definitions, which you may also find useful to provide clarity in your procedure:

- "Shall" expresses a requirement, as in "All sales calls shall be documented in the system."

- "Will" expresses simple future tense, as in "The new raised flooring will provide easier access to wiring."

- "May" expresses permission to choose a given option, as in "All employees may select from among three retirement savings plans."

KEEPING IT FLEXIBLE

As you document the procedure, keep *Rule S* in mind at all times; don't include a level of detail that won't add value to the procedure. You want people to perform the same tasks, in general, but do you need them to do every aspect of each task in the same way? If not, don't dictate the parts that don't have to be standardized. (As you may have noticed by now, the general message of this book is: "Think about it, and don't do more than you need to.")

It may also be true that you need to standardize some aspects of a task but that they can be done in two or more ways depending on local conditions. In this case, you can say so. A good analogy might be a recipe (which is also a kind of procedure) that says something like "Add two cups of milk; you may choose to substitute skim milk, soy milk, or almond milk." In a similar way, a work instruction may permit the substitution of interchangeable parts, or an office procedure may allow a task to be performed by either of two different roles, stating only that the person in the other role has to be informed that the task is done.

AVOIDING AUDIT TRAPS

Audit traps are unneeded words and rules in procedures that are not executed and that can thus result in an audit finding. One reason for keeping procedures as flexible as possible is to avoid audit traps; these are particularly annoying because they are traps you build to catch yourself. An old slogan for ISO 9001 is "Say it, do it, prove it." This applies to other standards, codes, and rules, as well as to customer expectations. The flip side of the slogan is "If you can't prove you've done it, then don't do it; if you won't do it, then don't say you will."

As you write your procedure, consider what records should be kept to prove that the process was executed and (for your own monitoring rather than for compliance to a standard) to show how well the process was executed. Think about human nature and your company culture, and do not commit your company to any actions that either don't need to be performed or that you know will not be performed.

CHAPTER 9

Finalizing Your Procedure

ONCE YOUR PROCEDURE is drafted and seems to be correct, as far as you can tell, you have just a few things left to do to get it ready to be launched in the real world. Launch planning is dealt with in detail in Chapter 10, but it needs to be started before the procedure is released. In fact, for efficiency's sake, you can start the planning now, before the procedure is even finished.

This is also when you make sure the draft procedure looks right—not just to you, but to everyone involved. Users involved in different parts of the process, suppliers, customers, and other stakeholders can all have very different perspectives. Send the procedure around for review, and revise it until your whole team believes that it's clear and correct. You may also want to run it by a few people who aren't on your team, to make sure it's clear to people who haven't been involved in all of your discussions.

Finally, publish the procedure to make it accessible to users, whether that's all users as you do a full launch or just a pilot group.

PLANNING YOUR PROCESS
LAUNCH AND FUTURE OPERATIONS

While the procedure author is creating the first draft, this is a good time for the rest of the team to begin thinking about how to deploy the process changes and inform people of the new procedure. If you begin creating your rollout plan now, you can be ready to implement your procedure as soon as it's complete. This is discussed more fully in Chapter 10, but the time to begin planning is now.

One item that must be considered right away is whether more procedures will be needed before this one can be launched. If you are working on a high-level procedure that defines what tasks need to be done to produce the desired output, determine whether you will need some lower-level procedures or work instructions that explain how the tasks are to be done. If so, then these also must be completed before the main procedure can be rolled out.

Ideally, your rollout plan will be done when the procedure is complete, or soon afterward. As soon as you are ready to begin implementing the procedure according to that plan, you will also need to have your control and monitoring plan in place, so that you can manage the process from the moment it's implemented. See Chapters 10 and 11 for more information on developing your rollout plan and control and monitoring plan, respectively.

REVIEWING AND REVISING
YOUR PROCEDURE DOCUMENT

Once your first draft of the procedure is completed, send it to the process team for review. It is most productive if you can get the team members to read through the procedure on their own. Each should create a redline (marked-up document) or a list of issues, which can then be sent to the process author or gone through at a review meeting with the team. Unfortunately, it is common to have people look through a procedure for the first time while in the review meeting, but that's not a good use of anyone's time. (One dramatic way to deal with this is to cancel the meeting and reschedule it after people have had time to read the document. However, unless this is a recurring issue, it's better and less likely to cause bad feelings if you just make the expectations clear from the beginning.) Because it's common for there to be conflicts among the feedback from different members of the process team, as well as from other reviewers, it is best to have at least one review meeting to discuss conflicts and reach compromises. A meeting might not be required when the procedure or work instruction is simple and there is general agreement on how it is to be carried out.

You may need multiple cycles of review and revision, especially for a complex procedure. Once the core process team agrees on the procedure, it is also a good idea to have others review it—particularly those who execute the procedure or who are directly affected by it, including internal customers for its outputs.

One special case is international companies. For a procedure that affects people who speak different native languages, you have two choices: (1) Get it translated (in which case you need someone to review and check the translation), or (2) expect everyone affected by the procedure to understand it in its original language. This is probably not a decision that's up to you; it depends on your company culture and on whether you have an official company language. However, you do need to take language and culture considerations into account when documenting and rolling out the procedure. Here are some factors to consider:

- If you get the procedure translated, try to get someone who is familiar with the process, the local conditions, and the local language to review the translation and confirm that it makes sense.

- If your company does everything in one official language, have the procedure reviewed by people who are not native speakers of that language. Depending on how fluent all of your people are in the official language, you may want to use short sentences with simple grammar. You should also try to avoid metaphors and figurative language, which can be confusing.

PUBLISHING YOUR PROCESS

After the process team and other reviewers agree that the procedure is complete and correct, it can be approved by the owner and any other approvers required by the process itself or by your process system. (Your Document Control Procedure should dictate how approvals are recorded and stored.) Then it's time for it to be released—placed under configuration control with the status of an official approved document, with a readable version made accessible to everyone concerned in the process. Once it's there, you can complete and implement your rollout plan.

At this point, the procedure is as good as your team can make it. What you now have is a procedure that has been agreed upon by its primary stakeholders and formally approved. It is published, so it can be accessed by others, but its existence has not yet been publicized to users. You may still need to test it or perform a pilot before you can be confident that it is as good as it can be. As with many models of real-world activities, the boundaries between phases of process change are not rigidly separated. I have chosen to end this chapter here, and to include testing in the next chapter, because the procedure has to be published before it is accessible to anyone involved in the pilot test.

Making Procedures Real

CHAPTER 10

Rolling Out Your Changes

THREE STAGES ARE CRUCIAL in achieving a well-functioning process, and documenting the procedure is only the first among three codependent equals. The other two are implementing the changes (which can also be called launching, rolling out, or deploying) and controlling the process in its normal operation (also called monitoring and managing the process). This chapter addresses implementation, and the next chapter covers process control. An unimplemented procedure is an empty thing, either killing trees to produce useless stacks of paper or taking up server space with useless folders and files; an uncontrolled procedure tends to work right at first and then gradually degrade.

Launching a new or revised procedure is a form of change management, and there are legions of books on that topic. This chapter discusses some aspects of change management that are specific to implementing process changes.

Here's a scenario that's all too common:

Kelly has been asked to take on the role of process owner for her company's time-reporting procedure, which everyone agrees has not been working well. Before deciding what improvements to make, she investigates the current situation and finds that only three years ago, a high-powered project team working with an expensive consultant developed a new process for employees to report their labor hours. Kelly obtains a copy of the team's new process, and as she reads through it, she finds her jaw dropping with surprise: It's an excellent process, containing most of the improvements she's been considering and a few she hadn't thought of. So why aren't employees using it? And why has Kelly herself—a process-minded person who's been with the company for two years and who has to report her own hours weekly—never heard of the process?

By this time, the consultant is long gone, and the project lead has moved to another unit of the company. Kelly eventually manages to track down Fritz, who was a member of the project team. She asks him why the time-reporting procedure was never used. He answers, unhappily, "I don't know! They use it in Spokane, where we had the pilot. They love it there! We told all the other site managers to start using it. Maybe it's because IT pulled the plug on the software that was supposed to go with the system, but even then, they can still use the process without the fancy tooling—just use a spreadsheet to log their time!"

Kelly digs a little further and concludes that Fritz and the rest of his project team did a good job revising the time-reporting procedure, but they made some major—and very common—mistakes in rolling out their changes:

- They ran a successful pilot, but then they assumed that everyone knew about it, even though there was not actually all that much communication among sites. The team worked closely with the pilot group, but they didn't realize how much of the pilot group's success was due to that intensive communication. The project team assumed that a simple email was enough to "turn on" the process in the rest of the company.

- They communicated with the wrong people, in the wrong way. At Kelly's company site, managers receive an average of 100 emails a day, and they quickly learn to filter them and ignore all but the most essential operational items. Furthermore, site managers don't have daily contact with most of their site employees; the supervisors one or two levels down are the ones who most influence employees' daily actions. In the case of the new time-reporting procedure, the site managers paid even less attention to the new system because it didn't influence them personally. They are indirect employees (meaning that their hours are billed to an overhead account rather than directly to a customer) and thus were not required to use the system themselves.

- The team communicated the wrong information. All of the training they provided was about using the new tool to report labor hours. But the tool wasn't yet available (the pilot team used simple spreadsheets instead), and as it turned out, the tool never did become available. Even those people who did hear about the new process had no understanding of how to perform the process without the special tooling. And because there was no pressure from management to use the tool and no explanation of the advantages of the new system, they were not motivated to figure it out.

Kelly continued to study the existing situation, and she decided that she needed to make only a few simple adaptations to the previous team's procedure. However, she was determined to add two other "legs" to make sure the process "stool" was firmly supported: She assembled a cross-functional team including people with knowledge of the issues with time reporting, as well as a good understanding of the process users and their work environment. In addition to the procedure itself, Kelly and her team created and implemented a rollout plan and a control and monitoring plan to make sure that, once in place, the new process was functioning as desired.

KNOWING WHEN TO CREATE A ROLLOUT PLAN

A *rollout plan* defines actions needed to launch a new or revised procedure. If you were to draw a process flow of the actual work to create a procedure and put it into effect, it might look like a simple loop, as in Figure 10-1. This is a correct view, in that the outputs of one process step become the inputs of the next. However, it also gives the misleading impression that the steps need to happen in a rigid, separated order. If so, it would be inefficient. It might also become ineffective if your process stakeholders help document the procedure but then are pulled back to other work and are not available to help with implementation.

FIGURE 10-1 High-Level Process Creation Process Map

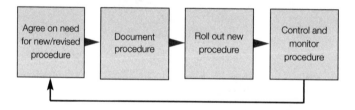

Instead, it is good practice to plan your implementation before you finish the procedure documentation. You don't need to have all the details ironed out in order to know what you need to implement a procedure. In fact, it may work the other way: Figuring out the implementation may provide some feedback that might improve your procedure as you finalize it.

By the time you've done the first draft of the new procedure—or maybe even before then, once your team has determined the process goal, scope, process flow, roles, and responsibilities—you have enough information to begin creating your rollout plan. Then, you can refine the plan as you review and revise the procedure and be ready to implement the procedure as soon as it's complete.

There are three necessary parts in your rollout plan: strategy, infrastructure, and communication. The essential input for all of these is a thorough understanding of the situation into which you will be launching: your company structure, its culture, and the current ways of working, plus the mindset, receptiveness to change, experience, and education of the population you need to address.

By the way, the term "rollout plan" is meant to be descriptive—not mandatory. Call it whatever will help the idea gain acceptance in your company. You can call it a "deployment plan," a "procedure implementation document," or whatever. Call it "George," if you like—what matters is to find a term that you and others are comfortable with.

DEVELOPING A STRATEGY

Strategy refers to strategic decisions about the structure of your rollout itself. Base your decisions on the needs of the process changes, as well as your knowledge of your organization and the people who will be involved in the rollout. How much training will be required? How long will it take to get any required tooling in place? How amenable are your people to change? The decisions to be made include the following:

- Do you want to implement your process changes all at once, or will you introduce changes in stages? There are advantages and disadvantages to both. A phased approach may cost more but introduce less upheaval than a big onetime change, while a onetime change can be upsetting to your organization but avoids the risk of having your management change its collective mind midstream.

- Do you need to enlist local champions, to spearhead the rollout in their own areas?

- If multiple sites or departments will be affected by the change, do you want to bring everyone on board with the new process at once, or do you want to deploy the changes to one group at a time? The best answer here depends on the size of the population affected by your changes, the culture of your company (and how accepting it is of change), and the resources available to deploy your new process.

- Do you need to test your changes? If you're making only a small change, this may not be needed, but if you're making changes that will have a high level of impact (whether by affecting lots of people, requiring expensive tooling, or making dramatic changes to ways of working), you might want to do a simulation of the new procedure or test it in the real world by running a pilot before you roll it out to the rest of the company.

Running a Pilot

For very large or complicated changes, it is common to run a pilot test, by launching your procedure to a small group early on. The procedure can be tested at one site, in one department, or on one product—whatever makes sense. Then, after that real-world experience shows you where your procedure needs to be improved, you can go back and fix it before releasing it on a bigger scale. If you run a pilot like this, you can also ask some of the people involved in it to review the changes to make sure their opinions and experiences are captured.

Piloting a process change can show you where you need to make improvements, not only in the procedure itself but also in the training you provide to your users and in the process infrastructure. Be careful, though; conditions in your pilot probably won't be an exact match for conditions in the full operation of your process. For one thing, you will probably be in closer communication with the people involved in the pilot than you will be later on with all process users. There may also be different conditions among the groups who will be using the procedure, because of location, culture, previous training, experience level, or a host of other factors. These may mean that the process runs differently in the full-scale deployment than in the pilot.

Caution: If you do decide to run a pilot, remember that the global rollout to follow it will need many more resources than a small pilot, because you'll need to communicate the same information and develop the same infrastructure for many more people. Don't be like Fritz's team in the example involving Kelly near the beginning of this chapter and put all your attention on the pilot; remember that it's only the prelude to a bigger challenge.

Incorporating Other Methods of Process Testing

Other methods of process testing depend heavily on what your process is. If you don't want to do a full pilot, it may still be possible to simulate the process by doing a dry run through it—using the tools, filling out the forms, testing the machines, or even role-playing for a process that's heavy on human interaction.

If you have developed new tooling, it is particularly important to test it on real users. In his books and on his website, usability guru Jakob Nielsen stresses that, while there are principles you can follow, there is no substitute for actual user testing. While his field is software, I think this applies equally to hardware tools; users find new ways to use (and misuse) your tools that you can't anticipate during development

In general, the more closely you can simulate real life in your process testing, the better. What seems perfectly feasible in theory is all too often cumbersome, annoying, or even impossible in practice, and it's better to find this out as soon as possible.

BUILDING THE NEEDED INFRASTRUCTURE

Infrastructure can include tooling, facilities, and support personnel, so it is individual to each process. Getting the infrastructure in place is basically a project management challenge; you need to develop a plan for what tasks need to be done, when they will be done, and by whom. One aspect of the plan that is specific to process rollout is that you need to time the infrastructure tasks together with the communication tasks, to make sure that they happen together. If you roll out the tooling before the training, you run the risk of people beginning to use it wrongly and getting into bad habits. If you train people but they can't execute the new process because tooling or facilities aren't yet in place, you breed frustration and run the risk that your people will forget what they've been taught.

COMMUNICATING PROCESS CHANGES

Communication of the process changes can include both training and information transfer. The central question you need to answer is: "Who needs to know what, and what is the best way to tell them?" Again, the answers to this depend on your knowledge of the people involved and your company culture. How are your people used to getting new information? What information channels do they pay attention to? Whom do they trust? How receptive are they to change? How well do they understand the big picture of your company's needs?

You probably have multiple groups, and each needs different information about the process:

- *Process users* need to understand what has changed—and why. Here is where human nature comes into it. It's possible to get people to follow a procedure blindly, through heavy use of authority, but at best they then work as automatons, following the procedure whether it works well or not. At worst, they passively resist by simply ignoring the new procedure. But if you can get them to believe in the need for the changes, they may follow the process intelligently and even suggest opportunities for further improvement. There may also be different groups of process users who require different training. For instance, in a salary procedure, the people who process the payroll need to know more than the people who receive their own pay. (In this example, the people in the payroll department are *also* salaried employees, and they need the same information everyone else receives in addition to their own specialized training.)

- *Process users' managers* need to understand what has changed and why. They also need to understand why it is important for their people to follow the procedure and what their own responsibilities are in making that happen.

- *Process customers* are those who make use of the process outputs. They need to understand whether anything has changed in the makeup or quality of those outputs, or in how and when they are delivered.

- *Process suppliers* provide the inputs to the new process. They need to know if there are any new requirements for them. (This should have been negotiated during the process creation, but if you worked with their management or with a representative sampling rather than with all suppliers, you may still need to do some training.)

Once you have determined who needs to know what, the challenge is to deliver that information—and in a very large company, that challenge can be formidable.

When you change a process that affects a small group of people, the communication is easy: Do it in person. Go tell them what's changed and why, and tell them as much as they need to buy in to the change. Provide them with reference materials and training as needed so that they can look up the answers to any questions when you're not around.

However, when you need to communicate to a large group of people, especially a group that is scattered around the world, communication is more difficult. You have a number of options; since each has its advantages and disadvantages, you will be most effective by delivering your message by more than one channel.

Email

Your quickest, easiest, cheapest, and (usually) least effective option, email is appropriate when you need to notify people of changes that won't really affect the way they do anything right now. Here are some examples:

- "We would like to inform all employees that we are changing the start page of our intranet. From now on you will see news stories relevant to our industry on the front page, and you can find a list of useful links for our corporate tooling in the left sidebar."

- "This is to let all administrative assistants know that we are introducing a new tool for scheduling our larger conference rooms. We will contact you directly within the next month to schedule training in the use of the new tool."

- "To all Customer Service Engineers: We in Logistics would like to inform you of our upcoming process changes. There are no requirements from you, but we expect the new process to provide your parts on time 99 percent of the time with a much lower breakage rate."

That last example might be a bit surprising. Why bother to inform people of a process change if all they have to do is to sit back and reap the benefits? The reason is that perception lags behind reality. People have developed their opinions of your processes over time, and even if you make a dramatic improvement, it generally takes them a while to notice the change and to believe that it's not just a fluke. If you notify them that something is changing, they may notice the changes sooner—and stop complaining about past problems more quickly.

People are more likely to read emails that are directed to them specifically than to read mass emails. If, as you develop a process, you develop contact with local managers, it might be more effective to communicate the changes to them and have them communicate with their people. If you do this, make sure that the management responsibilities for spreading the word are clear, agreed upon, and (ideally) enforced by higher management.

Teleconferences

The dynamics of a teleconference change a lot depending on the size of a group: You can do more intensive training when there are only a few participants. For processes that involve a lot of computer use, it can sometimes be better to use a telecon even when you're training only one or two people, because then all the participants have their own screens and can see clearly what's happening.

When you're training a larger group, try to make sure that only one person is speaking at a time. Make sure you provide backup materials so that people can look up anything they forget later. Realistically, half your audience is likely to be checking emails or doing other work during the call.

Computer-Based Training

Computer-based training (CBT) is a cost-efficient way to train a large group. However, it's easy for people to hit the "Next" button while not paying much attention to the screen. For a CBT to be effective, you need to motivate people to pay attention. You can do this in two ways, and you can do both of them together. First, make sure people understand why this change matters and how it will benefit them or the company. Convey this message by a separate email or announcement, or in the very beginning of the CBT. Second, add consequences for not taking the training. If possible, use a system that tracks who has taken the CBTs, and report those results to the managers who have the responsibility to make sure their people are trained. For very important process changes, add a test to the training and don't give credit until the test has been passed. Don't try to make the test tricky: That will just annoy people needlessly, for no real gain. Instead, ask questions about the fundamental knowledge they need to have of the process. That's what you want the to know!

In-Person Training

Conducting training in person is expensive, but it may be required for critical or especially complicated process changes. Depending on the size, makeup, and locations of the people to be trained, you can either have a single trainer (or small group) conduct all classes, or train a bigger group to go out and pass the training on.

Road Trips

By "road trip," I'm talking about having one or a few trainers conduct training for all of your user population. If all of your users are at one physical site, this is obviously a good choice, since no actual travel is required. If you're training a more widespread group, there are advantages and disadvantages. The advantage of having all training conducted by your foremost experts is that the students get the most knowledgeable teacher, who is able to answer all their questions. The disadvantage is that if you are training a widespread national or international group, much travel is required and the training may take some time, since only one class can be conducted at a time.

The Train-the-Trainer Approach

A method that can work well for training a large, diverse, or widely located population is to train a group of key people, who can then return to their own sites or departments and deliver the training. The advantage to this method is that these people (if you choose the right ones) understand local conditions and already have credibility in their home departments. If they believe in the change you're making, their coworkers may be more willing to trust it because they trust their trainers. These trainers may (should) already be experts in the process area, too, and can offer a lot of insight into the best way to conduct the training.

The disadvantage is that these trainers know only what they've been taught; they are not steeped in the new process in the same way as the process team. This is not a problem in many cases, but it might become one if you're introducing a very complicated new tool or way of working and the trainers can't answer questions from their students.

The Management Chain

Some processes do not need any actual training. All you need to do is say something like "There's a new procedure; here's where you can find it and you're required to follow it," or "We've had a few ways of working on this task in the past; from now on we're using this one, and you can find the documentation here." In this case, the best way to spread the word is to get management to buy into the change, and then have each manager communicate the change and the new responsibility to her direct reports, on down the company hierarchy.

This is extremely effective because the person communicating the changes is the same one responsible for making them happen, but it works only if you can get your managers (at the top level you're communicating to) to really believe in the usefulness of the change. Ideally, you develop a relationship with the critical managers, discussing what changes have been made and why. If you have not done this, then communicating via the management chain can fail dismally, as in the example of Kelly and the time-reporting procedure at the beginning of this chapter. Managers are not likely to tell their people to do anything differently based on an email from a process team they don't know, doing work they weren't previously aware of.

A Multipronged Approach

Given that each of the methods listed above has advantages and disadvantages, in most cases when you're making more than a minimal change, the most effective plan is to use more than one method of communication, using infrastructure and strategic decisions to support the rollout and create a climate in which it is a natural and expected thing to follow the new procedure. Let's go back to Kelly and the time-reporting procedure from the beginning of this chapter:

Kelly knew that the rollout of her process would be crucial to its success. She had the backing of upper management, and she knew she needed to leverage that to make change happen. However, she also realized that to make change stick, she needed to make sure people believed in the need for change—and she needed to make the new behavior easy for them. She ran a pilot, analyzed the results, and adapted her process. Then she worked with her team, management, and IT and came up with a plan.

An email was sent out to the entire company to let everyone know the new time-reporting procedure was coming. Upper management was asked to make it clear in their staff meetings that all direct employees (those whose hours were charged to customer contracts) were to use only the new procedure to report their labor hours. Upper management instructed all of their direct reports to cascade the message down to their own staffs, and so on down the management chain.

(Continued on next page)

The population to be trained included more than a thousand people, and the new procedure and tooling were relatively simple, so Kelly and her team decided to create a computer-based training. They asked IT to set it up so that after two weeks, supervisors received a report listing how many of their people had taken the training. Kelly's team also received this report, so they were able to enlist management help in getting the stragglers to take the training.

Because Kelly and her team also wanted it to be easy for people to follow the new procedure, they made one more request to IT, and since the new system was important to upper management, the request was granted: When any direct employees shut down their computer or put it into hibernation at the end of the day, they were greeted with a pop-up window that said: "Do you need to log hours?" If they clicked the "Yes" button, the new tooling opened up, and then shutdown proceeded once logging was complete.

In this example, Kelly and her team were lucky: Upper management already saw the need for their project. Kelly and the team didn't have to sell the benefits of their project; all they had to do was convince management champions that the new procedure and tooling would indeed produce the desired benefits, and educate managers on their own role in making the new process operational. On the "bottom-up" side, no one was particularly attached to the old system (because time-logging is always an annoyance and at best a necessary evil), but no one was particularly eager to have to learn a new system, either. The team used their email and their training to make it clear that the new procedure was more streamlined and more accurate than the old one, resulting in less time wasted for the employee and more profits for the company.

As previously stated, you may need to use different methods to communicate to different groups. For instance, you may need: a single slide to update top management, delivered at a monthly reporting meeting; a teleconference for team leaders explaining their responsibilities and the reasons for the changes; a CBT for process users; and a two-hour in-person class for key users who will be consulted whenever others have issues with the process.

CREATING EFFECTIVE TRAINING

Training is another topic on which entire books are written, so I'm confining myself to discussing some specific points that are relevant to process change. No matter which method you use to communicate your process changes, you need to have some kind of training material. This can be anything from a simple email message to complex slides used in classes, CBTs, or Webinars. No matter what the format of your training, it's essential to consider your material from your audience's point of view. Think about what they need to know and at what level they need to know it. Plus, just as with the procedure itself, it's a good idea to get the training materials reviewed by some of the people who will be using them, in order to make sure they are clear, complete, and comprehensible to your audience.

At this point, you and your team are experts in the new process. Your process's soon-to-be users are not: They may be experts in the subject area and in a previous version of the process or they may be completely new to these tasks, but they are definitely going to be new to the changes you're making. That means that you need to be very careful about how you communicate to them because once people thoroughly understand an idea, it's actually difficult for them to remember a time when they didn't know it. As an expert on the subject, you will be tempted to make unwarranted assumptions about what your audience knows and to give complicated explanations of details your audience doesn't care about. Try to avoid this: Use clear language and practical examples, and if possible, have your material reviewed by a typical representative of the process users you'll be training. Also, if you have multiple audiences, as discussed earlier, customize the material for each one.

Another factor to consider is whether your audience needs to be convinced or only educated. If they have an attachment to the old way of working, or if they are averse to change, you need to get them to buy into your changes by explaining why this process improvement was required and what issues will be fixed. If possible, keep this very concrete and explain how your audience's own work will benefit from the changes, as well as how the company will gain. On the other hand, if your audience does not have any particular problem with making this change, it will be frustrating and boring for them to have to read or listen to a string of arguments they don't particularly care about.

As with the procedure itself, try to avoid abstruse language, and explain any special terminology. Keep the training as short and informal as you can: Tell people why you changed the process, where they can find the new procedure, and how to follow it (including any training needed on new tooling). Offer as much background as they need— but avoid needless details that will only be forgotten (or worse, that could crowd more important points out of someone's memory). Figure out the crucial points you're making and make those memorable by the use of stories and vivid examples.

DEALING WITH VARIATIONS IN CIRCUMSTANCES, CULTURES, AND LANGUAGES

Throughout this book, we've talked about the importance of understanding your company and your people, so that you can tailor your procedure and roll it out in a way that will work for your business. Don't overlook the possibility of variation within your company, and don't assume one homogeneous plan fits all. People following the same procedure may need to execute it in widely varying circumstances; this may be because of the nature of their customers, local culture, or even language variations. Consider whether you need to vary your strategy, infrastructure, or communication to fit the varying users of your procedure.

If you are deploying your process to an international audience, you need to think about the same considerations for your training materials as you did for the procedure itself. Do you need to have it translated? If so, find someone who can review the translation against the original and who understands the changes you're trying to make. If it will be in a single language, will it be read by a large number of people who are not native speakers? In this case, it's a good idea to have your training reviewed by one or more people whose fluency isn't among the best at your company, in order to make sure your materials are clear.

IMPLEMENTING YOUR PLAN

Your rollout plan should be complete when your procedure is done, approved, and published, or reasonably soon thereafter. By "complete," I mean that you've decided on the strategy of your rollout plan, figured out what infrastructure you need to put in place, and determined what information needs to be conveyed to whom and how to do it.

Before you execute your rollout plan, you also need to have your control and monitoring plan completed (see Chapter 11). That way, you can begin to monitor the operation of your process as soon as it begins running.

Project management skills are strongly required for successful execution of a rollout plan. Often, processes are developed by people who are experts on processes, content, or quality in general, or by those who are mostly involved in daily operations of the process. These people may or may not have project management skills. If no one on your team has the needed skills, and if your rollout will be complicated, it might be a good idea to ask for help. Tracking the execution of your plan lets you know whether your rollout is sticking close to schedule and whether all planned tasks have been completed. Otherwise, you run the risk of an incomplete deployment, or of one so delayed that people lose faith in the procedure.

ASSESSING YOUR RESULTS

If your company has internal auditors, you may want to consider inviting them in once your process is complete for an informal audit. Internal auditors should be partners, rather than bogeymen; they can help you to figure out how well your process is working and where you need to make improvements. (Be careful of your language in order to help build this viewpoint. If employees in your company tend to think of an audit as a big scary test, you might want to call this an "assessment" instead.) This is a good opportunity to use the auditors' skills to assess how well your rollout went. They can make sure the new or revised procedure is operating properly.

Otherwise, you and your team should take this opportunity to do your own checkup among the process users. You should be looking for the following things, now that the procedure is in place:

1. Do people know where to find the procedure document?

2. Are they following it every time they execute this process?

3. Are records being kept properly (as defined in the procedure)?

4. Are KPIs being monitored and reported?

5. Is someone paying attention to the KPIs and taking responsibility for reacting to them when needed?

6. Is any part of the process a big problem for the users? Do process users have problems or ideas for further improvement that they'd like to discuss with you?

This is also the time to do a wrap-up with your process improvement team. Get the group together to assess the lessons learned from this project. What went well? What could have gone better? Did you notice any issues or opportunities during this project that ought to be considered in relation to related or similar processes? Document what you've learned so that it can be studied before undertaking similar process improvement projects in the future.

Then celebrate with your team! You've finished your project to create or improve this process, and now it's time to transition this procedure to normal operation.

IN-DEPTH EXAMPLE

Part V: Launching the "Process Improvement Process"

So far in our In-Depth Example, we've developed an example process improvement procedure—though as discussed earlier in this chapter, the process launch can be planned even before the procedure itself is completed. By the time we've done a SIPOC on a process, we know what the process goals are, who the users are, and what the existing conditions are—that's enough information to begin planning the process launch. For this example, we've assumed that the tooling required to map, document, and store a procedure and to deliver it to its users are in place so not much infrastructure is required.

It makes sense to do a pilot for the process improvement procedure. Perhaps one of the project team members, or someone else who has been interested in the project, owns a process in need of improvement. If so, that individual can use the new methodology to improve it, keeping track of what in the process works and if any changes are needed. At that point, the procedure has been proven to work; it can be revised as needed, based on the pilot experience, and finalized. (If very extensive changes are needed, you may want to revise the procedure and then do a second pilot.)

The one piece of infrastructure required is to put in place some process experts who can be consulted by process owners in need of help with their improvement initiatives. The steps needed to make this happen are to agree with management on who will fill this role, make sure that it is an assigned part of the experts' duties (with time allotted for the task), and then train your experts.

This new standard way to improve processes will need several different kinds of communication. A sensible choice might be to have multiple ways to deliver your message:

(Continued on next page)

- A short executive briefing (perhaps ten minutes long and including two or three slides) that can be delivered to alert upper management of the change

- A fifteen-minute CBT to alert process users of the change: reminding them that they are expected to follow the latest version of all company procedures and of where they can find those procedures; informing them of how to propose improvements for procedures they use; and letting them know how to request additional training if they become process owners

- A half-day in-person training for process owners on how to improve their procedures, with role-playing, concrete examples, and information on where they can get additional help, because if they need to improve a process six months from now they're not likely to remember everything they've learned

- In-depth training (lasting a day or two) for process experts, and an ongoing forum set up to give them a way to communicate with each other to pass on what they learn in practice

Once this information has all been delivered, we can declare victory, celebrate our success—and make sure that we know how the new process will be monitored and managed in its ongoing operations.

CHAPTER 11

Managing Your Procedure Operations

YOUR PROCEDURE is as good as you can make it and you've implemented it so well that all know exactly what they have to do, and all have agreed to do it. You're done, right?

Nope.

If you've done your job right in creating (or revising) the procedure and rolling it out, everyone will come in tomorrow and follow the new procedure. But what about next week? And what if you made a mistake, or the business changes, or there was some information that you didn't have, so that the procedure doesn't work as well as you expected? How will you even know, and how can you make a case to improve the process (again)?

That's why you need a *control and monitoring plan*, which describes how the process is measured, when action is needed, and what actions are to be taken. For this, as well as for your rollout plan, use your company's jargon or find a term that people are comfortable with. Sometimes the word "control" makes people nervous; in that case, you can call it a continuous improvement plan, a process maintenance plan, a procedure operations document, or a KPI plan—whatever works for you.

DESIGNING A CONTROL AND MONITORING PLAN

It doesn't matter what you call your control and monitoring plan. Likewise, the format you select doesn't matter, either. What *is* important is the information the plan contains. Any control and monitoring plan needs to include the following:

1.   What KPIs are being monitored

2.   Who is responsible for monitoring them and taking action when needed

3.   Frequency of monitoring

4.   What the expected values are

5.   What will be done if expected values are not met

See Figure 11-1 for one possible way to present this information.

Note that the term *KPI* is often utilized freely to denote almost any reported data used to run a business. In this chapter, I am talking only about process KPIs: data that tells you how well your process is working.

Badly selected KPIs, or an insufficient control and monitoring plan, may result in KPIs that are ignored, unnecessarily complicated, or used only for reporting and not as tools to drive action.

SELECTING AND MONITORING KPIs

As discussed in Chapter 8, KPIs are essential for controlling a process, and they need to be considered and determined when the process is created as an integral part of making it usable. However, as mentioned

FIGURE 11-1 Sample Control and Monitoring Plan

Process Improvement Process	
KPI	% of new processes created using correct process
How Calculated	100 * (# new processes created using correct process / Total # new processes created in past month)
Target Value	100%
Monitored By	Quality Systems Manager
Monitoring Frequency	monthly
Take Action If:	< 85% in first month, 95% in second month, 100% thereafter
Required Action	Contact owners of noncompliant processes, escalate to department heads if necessary
KPI	% of process revisions using correct process
How Calculated	100 * (# new processes revised using correct process / Total # new processes revised in past month)
Target Value	100%
Monitored By	Quality Systems Manager
Monitoring Frequency	monthly
Take Action If:	< 85% in first month, 95% in second month, 100% thereafter
Required Action	Contact owners of noncompliant processes, escalate to department heads if necessary
KPI	% of process users trained
How Calculated	100 * (# users trained to date / Total # process users)
Target Value	See targets per month shown on cashboard
Monitored By	Training Manager
Monitoring Frequency	monthly
Take Action If:	> 5% below target value
Required Action	Provide report to managers of untrained users

there, it may not always be desirable to *document* the full details of your KPIs within a procedure. For instance, you may wish to change what you're monitoring as your goals or business conditions change, or you may want to set new targets, so that if you include details, you will need to alter the procedure every time you want to redefine your KPIs.

As the process gets used in the real world, you may also find that you need to add some new KPIs, to provide visibility into how well the process is working.

Remember the following points when selecting KPIs:

- Keep them reality-based. Make sure the KPIs reflect real-world behavior, and make sure you actually have the ability to measure them. (This can be a particular problem when you're trying to measure existing processes, which may not be set up to be easily measurable.)

- Select KPIs that reflect the view of the (internal or external) customer(s), because ultimately, that's what matters to your business.

- Select KPIs that will drive the proper behavior from employees. (More on that later.)

- Select KPIs that can't be easily "cheated," whose values you can trust, that are measured in a clear and visible way.

- When possible, select KPIs that predict an issue before it becomes a serious problem.

- Avoid selecting too many KPIs or KPIs that are too complicated. As with procedures in general, keep KPIs to only what is needed.

When you institute procedures for monitoring, testing, or inspecting, you may also have process performance KPIs for other related procedures. These do not measure the procedure itself but rather use the procedure as a window into other areas of performance. One example would be a new inspection process that permits a company to find defects before a part leaves the factory. You would want to measure the process by looking at the ratio in defects found by inspection to defects found by the customer. However, this new procedure will also allow you to look at your defects overall, and make quality improvements upstream in the design and manufacturing processes.

Choosing SMART KPIs

SMART KPIs are those that are Specific, Measurable, Achievable, Relevant, and Timely. The SMART mnemonic is usually applied to goal definition, but the five attributes combined in this mnemonic can also remind you of the necessary attributes of a good KPI.

Specific

Consider what you are trying to measure as well as your reason for measuring it. The word "specific" in this context means that the KPI measures this process, without including unrelated factors. In the example of Kelly's improved time-reporting procedure from Chapter 10, a specific process adherence KPI would measure not the raw number of people reporting their hours (they might be using an old process) but the number doing so in the correct new format.

Sometimes process performance KPIs are difficult to separate out. In some cases, you may need to accept that a specific KPI reflects the results of two or more process improvements. For instance, a drop in part defects may be the result of both an improvement in the material selection process and an improvement in the design process.

Be creative. It can be difficult to create KPIs that measure only the effect of your procedure, so you may just need to exercise a bit of ingenuity. When that's absolutely not possible, report honestly: Make sure that the people you're reporting to understand what they're seeing and know all the factors that influence it.

Measurable

In order to manage according to data, as represented by KPIs, you want the KPI to be easy to measure and as objective and quantitative as possible. You don't want to choose KPIs that require many hours of work to gather measurements or that are completely impossible to measure. If possible, use data that is already being collected or that will be easy to gather.

For instance, in the case of a product you support, you might want to report your machine's reliability at customer sites (mean time between failures, or MTBF). This is feasible only if the machines are instrumented so that you can track exactly when they go down and when they're online again, or if there is a human observer who records that data. Furthermore, you might need permission from your customer, or a nondisclosure agreement, to collect that data and use it in your reporting; customers may be sensitive to the possibility of their production data being leaked to a competitor. Thus, when choosing a KPI, remember to check the following:

- Does the data exist? That is, is it currently measured or could it easily be measured with available systems?

- Is the data accessible to the person who's supposed to be measuring it?

Examples of good quantitative KPIs include number of defects per thousand parts (or per part—choose the scale that makes sense for your production quantities!), average time to complete a sale, and number of customer complaints per quarter. You can also have calculated KPIs, such as the ratio of the number of software bugs found during test to the number reported by customers.

Sometimes, you need to have a KPI that does not lend itself to quantitative measurement. Let's go back to Kelly and her time-reporting procedure.

To make sure her procedure is intuitive, easy, and quick to use, Kelly might want to measure the satisfaction of her internal customers—the users of the system. She needs the data monthly, but a monthly survey would inconvenience her customers more than the procedure could possibly make up for. However, a discussion with her tech support reveals that the reporting software has the capability to randomly add a question at the end of the report: "How easy was this system to use today, on a scale of 1 to 10?"

When you create hypothetical cases (like this one with Kelly), you are free to invent tooling capabilities to suit yourself. However, note that an even better-designed tool for Kelly might simply have measured and reported the average time it takes to do daily time-logging—an objective and quantifiable KPI.

If you use a subjective ranking, bear a couple of things in mind. First, it may be better to use a less granular rating system (e.g., use a scale of 1 to 5 instead of 1 to 10), because it can be difficult to differentiate between close ratings, as anyone knows who has ever filled out a survey and dithered over whether to report a service level as 7 or 8 out of 10. Second, it's a good idea to include a brief description of what each rating means to you, in order to decrease the subjectivity of the ranking.

Achievable

"Achievable" refers to whether the KPI's target value can possibly be achieved. We'll talk more about this later in the chapter in the section on target setting. The basic idea is that it's good management to choose a "stretch" KPI that drives improvement by taking some effort to reach, rather than one that is too easy or one that's impossible to achieve.

Relevant

Under the "Specific" category, we discussed the importance of finding KPIs that relate only to your process. Another factor in the relevance of a KPI is what exactly it measures. Make sure your KPIs are consistent with the actual goals of your procedure improvement and that they reward the behavior you want. As the adage goes, "You get what you measure."

The classic bad example is of a customer service center that rates its employees based on how quickly they can conclude customer calls and close tickets. The goal (presumably) is to satisfy customers in an efficient manner. However, this KPI rewards efficiency but tends to leave customers unhappy, feeling that the service person was trying to get them off the phone without actually solving the problem. To drive the desired behavior, the time metric needs to be supplemented by another KPI measuring customer satisfaction or number of problems conclusively solved. If these are not measurable, a reasonable substitute might be the number of repeat calls from the same customer (with a target of 0).

The other aspect of being relevant is: *Don't* measure anything you don't care about, and *don't* clutter your reporting and waste your time with useless information. If you never change your (or your company's) behavior or take an action if a KPI is off target, then there's little point in tracking it.

Finally, make sure that the KPIs are from the point of view of the customer of your process (who may actually be an internal customer). Measure what *he* cares about.

Timely

How often does your KPI change? How volatile is it? What is the delay in measuring? There's no point in reporting data every month if it changes only twice a year. On the other hand, for an extremely volatile average, you may want to report a moving average, most commonly taken over a four- or thirteen-week period. (That is, each week you would report the average of the data from the last thirteen weeks, rather than just showing the value from that week.) This allows you to view trends with less distraction from normal variation.

> Tricia wants to measure the effectiveness of her company's advertising, but she works at a small family-owned furniture company. Each item takes four months to produce, and the company sells only twenty pieces each year. It might sell none one month and three the next, just because of normal variation and seasonal patterns. Therefore, measuring the number of sales per month would tell Tricia nothing—she'd need to look at sales per year to see what's really happening. For her company, a better idea might be to monitor the number of calls or emails received, citing each advertising channel.

Another factor in timely KPIs is the idea of reporting leading data. In long-term processes, think about whether there are any indicators you can report that would provide warning in time to make corrections, if a procedure is going wrong. In Chapter 7, we talked about looking at the inputs and outputs of a process step, rather than a whole process. If you have determined that a particular step's input (or output) is critical to the quality of the procedure as a whole, then—if you can set a KPI to measure the quality of that input or output—you can predict problems with the execution of the overall procedure, possibly in time to fix it.

> Ling works for a large manufacturing company making medical devices. Because the company's devices can be life-critical, every defect found at a customer site requires a rigorous root-cause analysis. The results of this analysis are used to make further quality improvements in the company, so there is pressure to do the analysis quickly. Ling has been asked to improve the root-cause analysis procedure to make it more efficient. However, the improved procedure still takes four to eight weeks for each analysis. If Ling reports only the overall time each analysis takes, she won't have very much data, and what she does have will be reported too late to speed up a particular analysis. However, if she can divide the analysis into phases and report the length taken for each phase, she will be able to predict earlier which analyses are progressing slowly, and she may be able to divert resources or take other actions to speed up the slow ones.

Considering Which Types of KPIs to Include

Don't forget to include procedure adherence KPIs as well as procedure performance KPIs. The former can help you to understand the latter. *Procedure adherence KPIs* measure whether people are following the procedure. *Procedure performance KPIs* measure whether the procedure is having the desired effect—that is, are you reaching your goals? If not, there might be a number of different reasons for that. It's possible you simply didn't get the procedure right, but it's also possible that the procedure isn't being followed correctly. Think about what people will do differently if they follow the procedure compared to if they don't, as well as what artifacts will be created (checklists, records, and so forth). Then you can monitor those to see whether people are indeed following procedure, and you can take action if not.

It's also possible, though less common, that the procedure is not being followed but that goals are being met anyway. In that case, think about possible reasons. Maybe you can simplify the procedure. Maybe some users have an even better way of working and you can improve the procedure. Another possibility is that your procedure rollout raised people's consciousness and they are paying more attention to the task, even if they're not quite following the procedure. In that case, the improvement is likely to be temporary.

Setting KPI Targets

You can list KPIs within the procedure itself if you choose to do so, but don't list the target values of the KPIs there because they will change. Sometimes, you know from the beginning what you want your ultimate target to be (for instance, 100 percent of products delivered on time). Other times, you have to use your judgment to set an initial target (such as 5 percent cost savings relative to the same month in the previous year). In the second case, obviously, you want to fine-tune your target based on experience and set harder targets as you get better at following a procedure. Even in the former case, however, it can be better to set intermediate targets rather than shoot for that 100 percent from the beginning. It's better to set "stretch" targets that are hard but possible to reach rather than set impossible ones that run the risk of being ignored because of their impracticality. What you can do in this situation is set progressive targets. For instance, if you were at 40 percent of on-time delivery when you improved the project and you want to reach 100 percent, you set a goal of 60 percent for the month after the improvement and raise your target by 10 percent each month until you get to 100 percent. (Base the progression on your best judgment of what can be achieved, not on a smooth, arbitrary linear increase.)

Documenting KPIs

You need to document several attributes of each KPI: not only the target value but also the unit, "direction of good," and method of calculation. This ensures that the KPIs are computed in a consistent way and that everyone has the same understanding of them, which in turn allows you to understand what your KPIs are telling you and to have useful discussions about them.

A KPI can be measured by percentage or by another agreed-upon unit. "Direction of good" means whether it's best for the KPI to be higher, lower, or exactly at the target value. The method of calculating a KPI needs to be documented in order to ensure that it's done the same way every time. Often the description of a KPI can be taken in multiple ways, and it's not clear how it's computed unless you see not only the equation but also a description of what is and is not included. For instance, if you are reporting DOAs in spare parts (in other words, the spare parts that are "Dead On Arrival"—the parts that are found to be damaged at time of installation), are you reporting the number of DOAs encountered, the ratio of DOAs to spare parts delivered, or the ratio of DOAs to spare parts actually used? Are you including or excluding parts that were damaged by engineers during the installation process? Only when you have a precise definition can you be sure that you can do meaningful comparisons among KPIs.

Here are some examples of KPIs:

- For a new manufacturing procedure, your KPI might be "number of defects," with a target value of 0.001, where the unit is a simple number and the KPI is computed as (number of defects found) / (number of parts produced).

- For a new packaging procedure, your KPI might be the "percentage of products shipped that arrives with no damage." If you were achieving only 85 percent before instituting this new process, your goal might be 95 percent, but higher is even better. In this case, the unit is percentage, and the KPI is computed as (number of parts arriving undamaged) / (number of parts shipped).

- For that same packaging procedure, the receiving warehouse can track percentage of parts in the new packaging, compared to parts in the old packaging.

- For a trucking company that has a procedure governing how it schedules its drivers on long-haul deliveries, the goal might be to ensure both safety and efficiency. If the company (or the law) wants drivers to have at least twelve hours of rest before their next delivery, then twelve hours is the goal—much less is dangerous, much more is inefficient. In this case, the unit is hours, and the KPI would need to be computed such that it excluded days off and vacation time from the averaging.

Note that the first and second of these examples are procedure performance KPIs, the third is a procedure adherence KPI, and the fourth may reflect both performance and adherence.

Reporting KPIs

Once you have decided on your KPIs and their targets, then you can figure out how to make them visible. Who will collect this data? Do you want it reported directly by the process owner, or do you have data crunchers who will compile the data? Will it be reported weekly, monthly, or what? Will it be presented to management as part of a dashboard, or will it be made visible on a website?

For a lower-level procedure or one used by a smaller group, you might need the KPI to be visible only to the process owner or person monitoring the data. That person then has the responsibility and the span of control to take actions in case the KPI target is not met. (However, remember that one goal of a standard procedure is to avoid single points of failure. It is risky to have a KPI that's viewed by only one person. This leaves no way for that person's work to be judged, and if the person is ill or leaves the company, then you might have a failure that can develop serious consequences before it's even noticed.)

You may also choose to have a hierarchy, in which higher-level KPIs are reported to managers and lower-level ones are watched by process users to monitor their own part of the procedure (especially if the procedure itself has children procedures below it). This gets around a couple of potential problems on both ends. You are not cluttering up managers' desks with reports they don't really need to see. On the other hand, the lower-level KPIs can provide leading indicators to warn people about upcoming issues with the higher-level process. Also, occasionally top managers want to keep sensitive dashboards confidential, but in this way, the people who actually use the procedures can see what's going on with their work.

As usual, these decisions need to be tailored to your business and your specific process. Make sure that the definition of the KPI is clearly explained so that anyone monitoring or making decisions based on the KPI knows exactly how it's calculated and what it indicates. You can manage from data only if you understand the data.

TAKING ACTION BASED ON KPIs

The ability to take action is the entire justification for measuring the operation of a procedure; there is no point in reporting a KPI unless something is going to change because of it. This is why every KPI needs a defined target and "direction of good"—to help determine when action is required.

Ideally, a control and monitoring plan states the target value and describes what specific action will be taken if the KPI is more than a certain distance from the target. That may not always be possible; the person who is tasked to monitor the procedure may not have the span of control or the knowledge to take the needed action. Perhaps a cross-sectoral team is needed to analyze the problem or a higher-level manager is required to make a decision. In that case, you can still be specific about the immediate action to be taken. Rather than something concrete like "adjust the widget until the product coming off the assembly line is back in spec," the action might be "escalate through the following chain of command," or "create a team and follow the Root-Cause Analysis / Corrective Action Procedure."

Procedures are not forever. Remember that one function of a KPI is to let you know when you need to change the procedure again.

IMPROVING THE PROCEDURE

Your process KPIs are one of the factors that can let you know when something needs to change. There may also be changes to the business climate, directions from new management, or other opportunities for growth or improvement.

Improving Procedure Adherence

If your procedure adherence KPIs indicate that the process isn't being widely followed, you need to take actions to change the situation. The first thing to do is investigate why it's not being followed. To do that you probably need to ask several users directly. Try to find out if people object to something in the procedure itself, if they just didn't know about it, or if avoiding the procedure is perceived to be easier and free of consequences. The action to take depends on the results of your investigation. Common actions include the following:

- Communication and retraining help if people don't know about or don't understand the procedure, if they don't realize its benefits, or if they have misperceptions about it (e.g., it seems hard at first but is actually a faster way of working).

- Enforcement may help by adding consequences for not following a procedure. This generally means reporting the noncompliance to people in authority over the process users. I generally prefer to avoid this when possible and to try to get people to follow a procedure because they understand why it's there and agree on its value, but sometimes enforcement is needed.

- Changing the conditions so that the procedure is the only possible path is a great action, when it's possible. This comes under the heading of mistake-proofing, and ideally it would be part of the procedure development and deployment, but sometimes you don't completely understand the conditions until after the procedure is operational. An example here would be dismantling old tooling so that new tooling has to be used, though generally it's best not to do this until you've proved that the new tooling functions as planned.

Changing KPI Targets

If your procedure regularly meets or exceeds your targets, you may want to consider setting harder targets. This isn't true in all cases. If there's an exact number you have to reach (e.g., a packaging process meant to put twelve pills in a container has a target of twelve, and neither more nor fewer is better), or if your target is already as high as it can be (100 percent on-time delivery, zero safety incidents per month), then you can't change it. However, especially when you're trying to save time or money, you're ready for a new goal once you meet your existing target.

Improving the Process (Again)

Sometimes your KPIs and other procedure checks, such as audits or even user comments, indicate that your procedure simply isn't working as expected, or that it's not working as well as it could. Possibly the process improvement initiative failed, but it's also possible that it worked well but conditions have changed, or that new information presents a new opportunity. This is when it's time to start a new process improvement initiative and go through the whole Revise > Launch > Control cycle again from the beginning. Use the same methods as you did in your previous process improvement, but this time examine what happened last time, and apply the lessons you learned to make the procedure even better.

Reviewing the Skills Required to Make Process Improvement Happen

Facilitating Your Meetings and Workshops

THIS CHAPTER and the others in Part 5 of the book address some skills that are useful in many phases of improving a process or process system: facilitating meetings and workshops, driving change through your organization, and managing your process improvement initiatives.

Very often, when you're working on a process improvement initiative, other people have a higher level of expertise than you do in the area of the process you're creating. Even when you are an expert on a particular subject matter, you still need to get other people's viewpoints in order to ensure that a procedure balances the needs of all stakeholders. If you're creating or improving a process system, you may deal with upper management throughout the company and may need to balance a number of strong opinions. In all of these cases, whenever you bring a group of people into a room to work together, you need to do a lot of skillful facilitation, or someone needs to do it for you.

Facilitating is the art of getting knowledge out of members of a group and helping them arrive at a useful consensus. The difference between a meeting leader and a facilitator is that the meeting leader (or chair) calls the meeting, decides who should attend, and sets the agenda, whereas a facilitator directs a meeting to reach consensus, draws out quieter people and tones down more outgoing ones so that everyone's opinion is heard, and leads a conversation to a productive conclusion. The leader has knowledge of the subject and may want to drive the meeting to a particular conclusion, while the facilitator needs to act impartially.

It is possible to facilitate a meeting on a subject you know little about (though you do need to know enough to understand the conversation and evaluate the opinions offered). In fact, it may be more difficult to facilitate a meeting on a topic you understand well enough to have strong opinions on. While it's certainly possible for a chair to run some kinds of meetings without a separate facilitator, any workshop or meeting that requires brainstorming or the discussion of multiple viewpoints also requires facilitation. If the chair is doing it, she needs to make a clear transition to the facilitator role and guide the meeting without driving it. In general, for any meeting or workshop lasting two hours or more, it's probably better to have a separate facilitator.

Being a facilitator is a delicate balance: You need to be confident enough to stand in front of a group and lead a meeting that may include participants senior to yourself, while at the same time you need to be self-effacing enough to elicit other people's opinions without intruding with your own opinions. If you are not an expert on the subject being discussed, try to avoid offering your own opinions at all, except to push the group to clarify any wording that seems unclear. If you do have expertise on the topic, facilitating becomes a bit trickier: You need to express your opinion without raising it above those of others. One way to do this is to use the Socratic method, asking questions rather than making statements and thereby getting other people to voice the things that need to be said. Another option is to meet in advance with one or two meeting participants to discuss your concerns about the issue being covered in the meeting. Then those people can make sure those concerns are brought under discussion.

PREPARING FOR A MEETING

Every meeting requires some advance preparation; the longer and more complex the meeting, the more prep work is required. If you're the facilitator, meet with the chair ahead of time to discuss the agenda, making sure that you understand it and that enough time is dedicated to each topic. Make sure that you have everything you need for the meeting ready before it starts: slides, projector, screen, telecommunications setup, sticky notes, markers, whiteboard, whatever. Think about the goals for the meeting, what successful achievement of those goals will look like, and how you'll get there.

RUNNING A *GREAT* MEETING

One key to keeping your meetings and workshops productive is to discuss expectations from the beginning so that everyone knows who will do what and agrees on the intended outcome of the meeting. You can use the acronym GREAT to remind you and your group of the five aspects of the meeting to be discussed: Goals, Roles, Environment, Agreed-upon rules and Agenda, and Termination.

The first four letters cover items to be discussed at the beginning of the meeting, while *T* (for termination) is addressed in the last few minutes. The idea is not to spend meeting time on meta-discussions but to make the meeting more productive. If you touch on each of these topics *briefly,* you will find that a little bit of structure supports the rest of the meeting rather than bogs it down.

Goals

Every meeting or workshop exists for a reason, but if it isn't discussed explicitly, everyone may have a different idea of that goal, and most people are disappointed when theirs isn't met. Whether you've met to brainstorm the top-level model of a process system or to review the first draft of a new project, agreeing on the goal is the first step toward reaching it. If participants have different goals for the meeting, consider whether they all are compatible, and if not, have the group discuss the discrepancies and reach agreed-upon mutual goals.

Roles

Do you need to have someone taking notes of your discussion? In a workshop with several topics on the agenda, should you designate someone to keep track of time so all topics are addressed? If communication of results is needed after the meeting, who will take the responsibility for that?

The first time you structure a GREAT meeting, you will know who the facilitator is—it is the person in front of the room explaining the acronym. However, if you adopt GREAT or a similar structure as a standard at all important meetings, the acronym can also remind you to designate or elect an official meeting facilitator whenever needed.

Environment

This is where you share knowledge to ensure that everyone understands the logistical aspects of the meeting. Answer questions such as whether you will you be taking breaks at specific times, if coffee is provided, where the restrooms and safety exits are (if some participants are unfamiliar with the location of your meeting), any cautions about power cords that may be trip hazards, and so forth.

Agreed-Upon Rules and Agenda

As meetings get longer, it becomes increasingly important to agree upon rules in order to keep discussions productive. For a half-hour regularly recurring meeting, it may be enough to use the normally accepted code of conduct in your company's culture (for example, whether it's considered OK or rude to take a phone call during a meeting), but for a meeting longer than an hour or so, it's worth spending a few minutes to have the group decide on its own rules. Some common decisions include:

- *Phones.* Should everyone agree to turn off or at least silence phones and Blackberries? Should people be allowed to take calls but take them out of the meeting room?

- *Laptops.* Is it OK for people to use laptops during the meeting, or do you want to have them closed (except for the person who is recording meeting minutes)?

- *Questions.* During presentations, may listeners speak up to ask questions, or do you want all questions held until the end of a presentation?

- *Off-topic or unproductive speech.* Do you want to use a "parking lot"? This can be a large piece of paper taped to the wall or a page in the meeting notes. Whenever someone brings up a point that is important but that does not lead toward the meeting's goal, the facilitator can gently interrupt the person and list the topic in the parking lot to be addressed or investigated later, outside the meeting. (Caution: Don't put items in a parking lot unless you really are going to work on them later. Otherwise, you're disregarding topics that are important to a meeting participant, which is not a good way to win cooperation.)

- *Signals.* Do you want a way to end certain discussions? Some teams let any meeting participant use a signal, such as rapping on the table or saying the word "ELMO" ("Enough, Let's Move On"), to head off digressions or unproductive discussion. If the interrupted topic is important but not germane to the meeting, it can be listed in the parking lot; otherwise, abandon it and get back on topic.

The first part of the *A* in GREAT is agreed-upon rules; the second part of the *A* is the agenda. You don't need to go into detail, but let people know what topics are expected to be covered during the meeting and how much time you have budgeted for each. Verify that all agreed-upon goals that were just discussed can be reached via this agenda, and revise the agenda together if needed.

Termination

While the other items in the GREAT acronym are discussed at the beginning of a meeting or workshop, termination refers to the final wrap-up. Highlight any decision or conclusions reached by the group, in order to ensure that everyone leaves the meeting with the same understanding. If necessary, reiterate: "So we have come to agreement and will proceed in direction X." Agree on what happens next, such as writing up and sharing minutes, communicating decisions, and executing any tasks decided on in the meeting. Make it a real but tiny plan. A "real" plan is one in which every task has an assigned owner and an agreed-upon time frame, while "tiny" means that it can be decided in two minutes of discussion and can be documented in an email or sticky note, rather than anything formal.

WHEN (AND HOW) TO SAY "PLEASE STOP TALKING NOW!"

The central job of a facilitator in a workshop is to keep the conversation moving in a productive discussion and ensure that everyone is heard. This means asking questions or encouraging contributions from the quieter members of a group, but it also can mean applying the brakes to stop someone more outgoing from dominating the conversation. Sometimes this can be scary, if you have to interrupt the senior manager in the room, for example.

People may go off into extended rants (which may or may not be germane to the point of the meeting) because they're passionate about the point they're making, because they're worried that they won't be heard, because they are knowledgeable about the topic and used to being the authority, or sometime because they've just gotten carried away. In all cases, you need to assure people that they have been heard. One way to do this is by restating the major point they've made. If it's a major point that contributes to the meeting goals, write it down on a whiteboard or flip chart. If they're trying to provide details that are relevant to the point but not needed in the meeting, you can say so but assure them that the details will be addressed later. (Make sure this is true, perhaps by adding it to the list of tasks to be performed after the meeting.) Stress that you value the views being stated but that you need to make sure other people are heard also. (If necessary, you can say, "Of course, you're the authority on this topic, but the procedure needs to incorporate the other stakeholders' points of view as well.")

I find that you can get away with a lot, even when you have to stop a senior manager, if you keep your interjections brief, polite, and direct. Don't apologize. Try to make it clear that you're interjecting to keep the meeting on track—not because you don't value what the person is saying. Wait for the person to pause or, if you're at the front of the room, hold up your hand to signal that you need to speak, and then say something like "Thanks, Jim. I think Amal wants to add something—Amal?" or "That's an important point, but I don't think it gets us to [restate the goal of the meeting here]. I want to make sure it isn't lost, so let me write it down in the parking lot, and we can call a different meeting to address it with the right people."

In other words, you don't want to shut people up: You want them to stop talking, which is a very different thing. The best way to do this is to help them feel that they don't need to keep talking because their message has been heard and understood.

LEADING A BRAINSTORMING SESSION

Sticky notes are the facilitator's friend whenever you're leading a group in a brainstorming exercise (for instance, when you're trying to figure out the major areas in a business model at the top of a process system or the activities in a process). As previously described, give everyone a pad of sticky notes (or several notes) and a pen, and ask them to list each of their suggestions on a separate note. Give them five to fifteen minutes for this, with no talking allowed. Stick each note to a blank wall. Depending upon what you're doing, you can set up different areas for different types of suggestions and hang each note in the appropriate area, or you can just put them all up anywhere. If time and the number of participants allows, have one person at a time hang up his sticky notes, reading each one out loud; otherwise, let everyone hang up their notes at once. Then let people move the sticky notes around, grouping similar ones. Next, lead the group in discussion of each cluster. Get agreement to remove duplicates, and rephrase notes when needed for clarity or when one suggests an expansion to another. You will probably find that the discussion sparks a few more ideas, when one person's note reminds another individual of something that needs to be included.

If you don't have sticky notes handy, small pieces of paper and tape works, too. Or you can have people write ideas on a whiteboard, copying each one into a textbox on a PowerPoint slide (or drawing program) that you beam onto a wall, and moving them around as directed by participants. I prefer to have people do their own sorting, though. For one thing, it's easier for people to stay focused in a meeting when they can participate actively, and being able to get up and move around makes a bit of a break. Therefore, I'd lean toward the use of sticky notes or paper and tape in most cases.

If you're working on something like a process map where the order of tasks is important, you can then move the notes around on a whiteboard and draw arrows showing the path through actions in a process, until everyone agrees that the order is correct. Take a picture or number the notes and make a quick sketch of where each one goes. After the meeting, you can draw what the group has come up with in a more readable format and bring it to the next meeting so it can be reviewed for correctness.

FACILITATING FROM BEHIND

Sometimes, it's not your meeting and the person who is running it has chosen not to use a facilitator. In this case, you may still be able to use some of your facilitation tricks as a meeting participant. You can suggest meeting rules at the beginning, for instance. You can also drive the meeting wrap-up at the end by asking for a recap, with questions like: "OK, so what have we agreed to and what do we need to do next? Who will handle this task? Should I do that one?"

If you volunteer as scribe (taking meeting minutes), you actually have a lot of power to make the decisions clear. If you're not sure what a speaker has said, you can ask her to clarify and restate it in order to make sure your notes are correct. If you want to make sure you don't sound like you're trying to take over someone else's meeting, you can phrase any of these contributions as a question, like "Do we have a meeting agenda?" and "What are the major points we need to discuss?" Just be sure to listen to the answers. Remember that it doesn't matter if *you* say what needs to be said—it matters that it gets said.

Facilitation is a skill with a lot of applications in process improvement and elsewhere. Mastering it can help any time you need to make sure that a variety of opinions gets heard, and that meetings come to a fruitful conclusion. It is a critical skill when trying to pull information from people across your organization to create and improve upon business processes.

CHAPTER 13

Driving Change Through Your Organization

THERE ARE TWO BASIC STRATEGIES to implement a change within a business: from the top down and from the bottom up. Top-down change occurs when management says, "Make it so!" and everyone else implements the direction. Bottom-up change happens when the people who need to change their way of working do so because they believe that the change is an improvement.

The advantage to top-down change is that it can be relatively fast. Only the managers with power to set the new direction need to be convinced initially, and they can ensure that whatever resources are needed to make the change happen are funded: training, tools, infrastructure, coaching, and so forth. The disadvantage is that the change may never be completed. Especially if management has a history of pushing the "flavor of the month," employees may not believe that the change is needed or that it represents a permanent change in direction. If employees don't believe that the change will be an improvement, they may simply continue to do their work in the same way as they always have, trusting that no one will notice.

In contrast, bottom-up change can be slow but thorough: If you can convince people to truly believe in the change you want to make, then change will happen and it will stick. One downside is that it can take a long time to convince a large number of people that change is needed. The more evident a problem is to a group of people, and the more they feel the consequences directly, the easier it will be to convince them of the need for change. Another downside is that if management doesn't buy in, it can be difficult to get the infrastructure support needed to make change happen or to get access to all of the groups who need to change.

Top-down change can be efficient, but sometimes not effective; bottom-up change can be effective, but sometimes not efficient. I've believed for a long time that the most effective way to make change happen is to push it from both directions at once. One or the other direction may be more important, depending on how hierarchical your company culture is. Are people used to doing what they're told, or are they more self-determining? To what extent do employees determine how they do their own work? However, even in the most egalitarian, laid-back company, change still happens faster if managers make their expectations clear, if they reflect the new goals in their own behavior, and if there are consequences for not following procedures. Similarly, even in the most rigid hierarchy, if people don't understand the reasons for a change, or if the new procedure doesn't seem accurate and effective to them, they may passively resist by simply not following the procedure. That's why the best way to make change happen relatively quickly *and* to make it last is to use top-down and bottom-up channels at the same time.

MAKING TOP-DOWN CHANGE

In most companies, getting management support is largely about the bottom line: If you can prove that your change will save your company a significant amount of money—or time, which is money to a business—you can sell it to management. Smart managers look at the big picture, considering both direct and indirect costs. For instance, if you can save money in the short term but only by making employees so unhappy that many leave, then you will not save money in the long term.

The difficulty here is that not all changes can be easily translated to dollars. If you're working in a data-rich environment, it's easy. If you're manufacturing parts, and your new process reduces the time to make each one from four to three hours, you can compute the time saved by simply multiplying by the number of parts. Then you can convert time to money either by adding up the extra number of parts you can sell or by multiplying the person-hours saved by the average hourly wage. Subtract any costs for the process improvement (i.e., training or new tools required), and you have a business case.

On the other hand, if you're trying to reduce the time it takes to complete and submit a travel request, and you don't know how many travel requests are submitted in an average year, it's difficult to tell whether a process change would save enough time to be worth the costs of training employees in the new process and paying for any needed software changes. In my experience, you are more likely to succeed in selling your change proposal by estimating costs and savings for a business case, even if your estimates involve a lot of guesswork, than by reporting only nonquantitative benefits of a proposed change. To be fair and honest, you will need to explain the assumptions behind your estimate numbers, so that managers can make their own informed decisions about whether your business case is valid. It's a good idea to include the nonquantifiable benefits of a change as well, but only as an addition to a business case made in terms of hours or dollars. Even if your estimates are incorrect, you've provoked a useful discussion; you can then get management's inputs and direction and reformulate your business case.

In certain cases, dollars (or hours) are not the primary driver for a change. In these cases, you still need to make your case in quantifiable terms. Remember that binaries (yes/no answers) count as quantifiable measurements. By that, I mean anything that either permits the desired outcome or doesn't permit it, such as "If we make this change, we can get certified; if we don't, we can't." That "yes/no" outcome is also a form of measurement, and assuming that everyone agrees on the desired outcome, it's easy to make a convincing case.

The trickiest case is one where there is no objective data. In that case, you may have to resort to subjective data, though you can still quantify it. The most common example of this is customer satisfaction: It's purely subjective, but if you ask your customers how they feel on a scale of 1 to 10, you can at least come up with averages. In order to get the clearest picture possible, you'd want to break your questions down into specifics. You can ask about the quality of your products, the ease of doing business with you, the responsiveness of your organization, or whatever is appropriate. When you have known issues, you can also ask how customers would respond to specific changes, remembering to phrase your question from the customer's point of view. (That is, don't ask how much they care about whether you do a better job testing your purchased components. Ask how much they care about whether you can reduce dead-on-arrival products by 50 percent.) The best case, when possible, is to come up with creative objective measurements to replace subjective ones. For example, instead of asking how satisfied customers are, measure the trend in number of customer complaints. (You might need to break this down further because some customers always complain. However, if complaints of severe quality issues are being replaced with minor complaints, you know that customer satisfaction has improved.)

ESTABLISHING BOTTOM-UP CHANGE

Building change from the bottom up is not necessarily harder, but it is more complicated. Instead of trying to convince one or a few managers, you're selling your change to the whole process user population. It's usually a much larger group, and they generally have a wider range of concerns. In their excellent book *Switch: How to Change Things When Change Is Hard*, authors Chip Heath and Dan Heath make the case that in order to drive change, you need to address three things: the heads, hearts, and habits of the people making the change.

"Head" refers to the rational reasons for the change—the reasons you'd use to make your case to management. If your new procedure saves time or money, complies with regulation, or makes customers happier, you can convince process users' rational sides that your change is worth making.

"Heart" refers to the emotional reasons for the change. Sometimes this applies to business processes, as when you're making a change that just intuitively feels right, such as proposing that people doing the same process carry it out in the same way. (Be careful with this one: Emotions can be tied to doing things the way they've always been done, or to keeping each site unique.) It's hard to think of business processes as having much of an emotional component, but some relevant components are self-interest, pride in the work, and desire for recognition. If you can appeal to self-interest by convincing process users that the change will make their work easier, get them more recognition for their hard work, or give them a greater voice in areas of the business that affect them, you will have gone a long way toward getting them to accept the change. Most people really do want to do their jobs well, and if you can convince them that the change is an improvement (in terms of producing better quality or producing equivalent quality more efficiently), then you can appeal to their pride in their work. People also want to be seen as doing their work well. They're likely to do what they get rewarded for. Try to build a culture that rewards people for following procedures and doing their jobs right the first time, rather than for going to great lengths to correct errors. Remember these factors when you design and report KPIs. Make it visible to managers when their teams are doing well, and encourage them to reward good behavior.

Finally, there are "habits." (That's my word. The Heath brothers use a vivid metaphor involving an elephant driver, but you need to read their book for that.) This is another way of stating what I said in Chapter 6: Ideally, you need to make it easier for users to follow the procedure than not to follow it. Even if that's not possible, you can guide users through the procedure by changing their environment, using tooling, checklists, culture changes, management oversight, visible reporting of status within the procedure, mistake-proofing, and so forth. Help the users to follow the new path until it becomes habit and gains acceptance as "the new normal."

BUILDING TRUST
(OR "WHY SHOULD I LISTEN TO YOU?")

Very often, people who are trying to change procedures or implement new process systems are in a position of *influencing without power*—sometimes this is even a formal part of the job description. You need people to trust that when you're talking about how to do their work, you're going to get it right. The best way to build that trust is also the way to get things right in the first place: Listen to people, pay attention to what they say, and do what you say you'll do. Listen before you write any procedures down, and listen to feedback after you've written the procedures down so that you can correct any errors.

Sometimes people only want the feeling that they've been heard. This is part of building the trust that leads to influence. Sometimes people have insights into their own jobs or business areas that no one else has (sometimes not even their boss). In that case, you need to act as a facilitator to capture that knowledge and to get people talking to each other in order to reconcile any conflicting viewpoints. One of the best ways to overcome resistance to new processes or systems is to bring the people who are resisting them onto the process team. After all, these are the very people you want to include in your improvements: They know the process, they work with it, and they care about it (or they wouldn't be complaining). This is true even when you think their complaints are wrong, because they're pointing out a failure in how you communicated your changes, but it is much more strongly true when they're right. If they have the experience and expertise to pick out problems with your new process, they can also help you find and correct problems in the existing way of working.

OVERCOMING RESISTANCE TO CHANGE

Unfortunately, it's not uncommon to encounter people in your company who do not want to follow standard procedures. Sometimes they say so straight out—which is good because then you can understand their reasons and counter them appropriately. Sometimes they won't say anything and just won't follow the procedure, which is a more difficult situation because it can be hard to even see that there's an issue. If you do not already have a mature process culture in your company, you will encounter resistance to change somewhere (or everywhere) along the way. You need to deal with this at every step by listening to people and addressing their concerns.

There are some common reasons people give for not wanting to follow a procedure, and each of these has a different solution.

- **"That's not the right way to do it!"**

Sometimes, the criticism isn't with the general idea of procedures but with the specific one in place. The best solution is to get the procedure right in the first place, or to revise and correct an older one that is already in place. It is not absolutely necessary for the person writing the procedure to be an expert on the subject matter, but it is necessary for that person to involve and listen to people who are experts. Try to involve a variety of viewpoints: the person who creates the inputs, the user of the outputs, people who are affected by the working of the procedure. Most important of all is to include one or more people who will actually perform the procedure. This may seem obvious, but sometimes it gets overlooked when a procedure is mandated by upper management to be carried out by lower-level employees, or when headquarters dictates actions to be carried out in satellite offices. If different people will be performing the procedure under different circumstances, try to include a broad sampling to ensure that you make it sufficiently flexible to meet real-world needs.

If you get the procedure right, you cut down on complaints about it. You may still get some mistaken criticisms, either because the commenters don't understand the subject as well as they think or because they don't understand the change you've made. (In the latter case, your communication may have been unclear.) You can then point out all the experts who were involved, and then explain that the comment was carefully reviewed and why you still believe the process is correct. This may convince the commenters; if not, you will know that you need to start a discussion among the people involved, because either more training is needed or something actually was overlooked by the experts in creating the procedure.

- **"I don't have time for red tape. I need to do *real* work!"**

Sometimes people don't like procedures because they think they add a bunch of useless administrative work on top of the existing workload. The solution to this criticism is twofold, lying partly in creating the procedure and partly in rolling it out.

It is true, in fact, that many corporate procedures make unnecessary work. It's also true that many procedures contain necessary work that isn't understood by the people who have to follow them.

> As a young software engineer, I was appalled that NASA wanted me to write two documents and present them before I could write a line of code. I complained loudly about governmental red tape! Years later, once I'd learned more about systems engineering and quality, I realized NASA was actually just trying to make me follow a proper and sensible engineering process: Document your requirements, agree on them with the customer, create a design, verify that it meets the requirements, then produce your product. A little bit of explanation would have helped me understand the reasons for what I was being asked to do—and I'd have done a better job.

- **"I don't want a standard way of working. You're restricting my creativity!"**

This criticism is a lot more common than you'd think, especially among people (like designers or software engineers) whose work *does* require creativity. It's true that the creative part of their work cannot be standardized, but almost all assignments, at least those in the corporate world, contain routine tasks as well as creative ones. For example, once a design has been created, it needs to be documented and stored in a standard way so that it can be accessed, understood, and used by people other than the designer. Similarly, software code can be reviewed by an engineer's peers in a standard way, with review records saved. This process tends to lower software testing costs because some bugs are found earlier on in the process.

I hold a private pilot's license. When faced with the "creativity" objection to following processes, I like to explain that a pilot-in-training practices emergency landings over and over again, in order to ensure that the parts of emergency response that can be automated become routine. As a result, when faced with a real emergency, pilots are free to concentrate their attention on the parts of the situation that require creativity and attention—like getting the engine restarted or finding a safe place to land. In the same way, if you standardize the routine parts of a job, you're able to focus your creativity on the areas where it's actually needed.

I've even heard people object to the simplest standardizations, like using a certain format for headers in a software module. My answer was, and is, "Do you really want to spend your time and energy figuring out what to write in your header? Or if you're reading someone else's code, do you want to have to work to figure out who wrote it, when, and why? Wouldn't it be better to make those things obvious, so you can get on with the more interesting and creative parts of your work?"

- **"It's just a piece of paper. No one's going to follow it anyway!"**

Often, this is all too true. The solution to this problem is careful change management in both the top-down and bottom-up channels.

The top-down solution is for managers to make it clear that following procedures is an important (though possibly new) part of company culture, and that all employees are expected to understand and follow the procedures relevant to their work. The bottom–up solution is to create procedures that people can and will follow, and to educate them on the other advantages to following standard procedures: A standard way of working builds consensus and ensures that inputs and outputs are aligned across the business.

When setting up a process or even a process system, you may encounter resistance at various points, and it's best to begin getting buy-in from all stakeholders from your first contact with them. If you can get people to feel they are a part of the project team, even on the outer fringes of that team, and to feel a sense of ownership, they will go on to influence others with whom they're in contact, and you will see acceptance of your changes spreading.

CHAPTER 14

Managing Your Process Improvement Project

THE ACTIVITY OF PROCESS improvement is usually structured as a project with an initiation, a breakdown of tasks, a project plan, and (hopefully) a wrap-up at the end. Whether you're revising a process system or creating and implementing a new procedure, you have to plan and track your tasks and use of resources, and you almost certainly will be required to show accountability for them to your management. It takes the same skills to manage a project improvement initiative as to manage any other kind of project, and there are hundreds of books on the market about project management. Therefore, in this chapter, I just briefly discuss some specific aspects of project management that need special attention when running process improvements projects.

Four aspects of process improvement projects typically make it difficult for project leads to intuitively apply project management concepts. I address the solutions to these typical issues within a classic project management framework.

Problem 1: Defining When the Improvement Project Is Done

- *Issue:* Most companies want to foster a culture of continuous improvement. Thus, it can be difficult to predetermine and obtain agreement on the point in time when you can call the project done and successful.

- *Solution:* Clearly define the objectives of the initiative, establish the scope, and obtain agreement on the success criteria through stakeholder management. The section of this chapter called "Initiating the Project and Defining Completion Criteria" provides insight on how to set these project parameters.

Problem 2: Developing a Strategy to Plan and Align Simultaneous Project Activities

- *Issue:* As discussed in Chapters 9 and 10, many of the actions required for successful process improvement need to be done in parallel. Too often in process improvement projects, team members don't think about how the procedures will be rolled out until after the documentation is completed. This can result in a lack of information and communication during the project, leaving process users to invent their own spin on why the changes are happening, and can ultimately lead to a very difficult implementation.

- *Solution:* In the beginning of the project, develop a clear strategy and integrate it into the project plan. The section "Defining the Project Execution Strategy" later in this chapter discusses topics to consider in formulating a successful strategy.

Problem 3: Establishing, in Detail, How Improvements Will Be Achieved

- *Issue:* Process improvements are often communicated and tracked at a very high level. Activities in a project improvement plan can have vague titles like "Improve Process X" with a duration of a few months. This lack of detail is not only bad project management, but it also does not help the project team members understand what is required of them. Some team members and other contributors have never done process improvement projects before and don't really know how to achieve the desired results, which leads to floundering that uses up critical time before the project gets moving in a constructive direction.

- *Solution:* Create a detailed project plan that breaks down the work into clear, measurable pieces that can be completed by the people involved, and make these details available for all involved to use as a guide. The section "Creating a Detailed Project Plan" later in this chapter provides a level-of-detail target toward which you can strive and an example that you can use in your project.

Problem 4. Allowing for Iterative Process Improvement

- *Issue:* Most people want to jump in and fix a process in one fell swoop. This does not allow for incorporating the viewpoints of multiple stakeholders, for synchronizing changes to related processes that are being updated in parallel, or for learning valuable lessons during real-world testing of the process.

- *Solution:* While developing your improvement strategy, specifically include iterations into the project plan. Within the section on "Creating a Detailed Project Plan" later in this chapter, examples are included to show how iterations can be planned from the beginning and how these iterations can help improve the efficiency of your business. Each iteration requires additional levels of detail and should include checks to make sure that related processes work together efficiently. Those checkpoints are where you often realize significant efficiency gains in your business, since the review includes the latest information presented within a holistic view. Needed process adjustments can then be made with minimal rework because they are done in sync with the overall project.

INITIATING THE PROJECT AND
DEFINING COMPLETION CRITERIA

Spending a little time at the beginning of a project to think through its scope and objective, define a strategy, and build a detailed plan speeds up the overall project by making it run much more smoothly. Ideally, this is done during the initiation phase of the project, but if you find yourself getting bogged down as a result of lack of clarity, you can step back and rework these project elements at any time. They are the foundation of any project, and they should be reviewed periodically and updated as required throughout the entire life of the project. Each element is applicable to process improvement projects of any size, from improving a single procedure document to implementing a full business process system. The amount of work required scales up with the complexity of your project.

If you've never created all of these elements before, they can be a little daunting, and you might worry about the time needed to define them. However, with focus and practice, the elements can actually be defined relatively quickly. For smaller projects, it may be possible to define all of them in a few hours. For larger projects—such as creating a whole segment of a process system, including all related procedures—all necessary information can be gathered in a three-day workshop with a team of the required subject matter experts. The basic structure is as follows, though of course you can customize it:

- *Day 1: Define the scope and objectives of the project.* Planned results of this day are:

  - A clear list of in-scope and out-of-scope items

  - A single statement that clearly describes the project objective

  - A team of people who have agreed about their understanding of this project and what needs to be accomplished

- *Day 2: Create the project schedule.* Planned results of this day are:

  - A list of key project deliverables

  - A *work breakdown structure (WBS)*, which is a common, standard project document showing a hierarchy of project tasks, reflecting the strategy of the project

- A sequenced and linked list of activities to realize the deliverables
- *Day 3: Complete the project schedule.* Planned results of this day are:
  - Realistic durations defined for all identified activities
  - A list of ideal owners named for each activity
  - If time permits, a list of risks and mitigation activities identified and added to the project plan

It's best to hold the workshop over three contiguous days. If that's absolutely impossible to arrange, try to at least have them close together, with all three days occurring within two weeks or less. If you have too much time between days of the workshop, people are apt to forget previous discussions, and some will need to be reviewed or rehashed.

For the workshop to be successful, the proper participants need to be invited. These people should be selected based on the knowledge and experience that they can contribute to creating the plan. Each individual may or may not be directly involved in the project going forward. If your project is very large, you may need to hold a mini-workshop with a few of the key people in advance, to form an initial high-level strategy and to identify how you want to break out the work among small teams during the main workshop. In this way, each team can work out the detailed scope, strategy, and detailed plan for its piece of the overall program in parallel during the workshop.

As an example, consider Bill:

Bill is the manager tasked with setting up a new factory for medical products. Because this is a new business area for his company, and because different regulations apply, an entirely new set of procedures is required (though they will fit into his company's existing process system). Many of these procedures will interlock with each other as the product moves through the entire manufacturing cycle. Bill will be doing the overall program management, with a different leader for each process creation project within the program. He sets up a workshop with seventy people

(Continued on next page)

broken up into ten teams, each with its own subject matter experts focusing on one key set of deliverables within the project. After the workshop is done, his teams have produced an overall program plan as well as more detailed plans for each project, containing more than 10,000 activities that are scheduled over the next three years.

During this sort of workshop, a facilitator is required and should be involved in the preparations. As discussed in Chapter 12, a facilitator's job is to manage the discussion, keep people on topic, manage the time, actively make sure all participants are engaged, help to get and clarify information from the participants, and stay independent during the discussions. It is possible for one of the key contributors to serve as facilitator, if an external person is not available to do so. If so, it's important that this person avoid dominating the workshop with his own opinions.

Before conducting the workshop, or at its very beginning, you also need to establish a clear project governance structure so that once you're done you can get formal approval for any decisions made during the workshop. A *governance structure* defines who has the authority to make final decisions for the projects. For example, who needs to give final approval for a decision on the scope and goals of the project? Typically, this is done by a project board, which is a group of managers who are key stakeholders of the project and who meet at a regular frequency. Their meetings should be rather formal with published minutes that record the resulting decisions and the actions defined within the meeting.

Defining the Project Scope

The first common problem with process improvement projects is that they sometimes lack a clear definition of when the project is done. To avoid this, a clear project scope must be defined and the project completion criteria need to be agreed upon.

The *project* scope is distinct from the *process* scope discussed in Chapter 6. The process scope defines what the process will do, while the project scope defines what work is required to create/update the process. The scope of a process dictates what business activities the specific process needs to include, whereas the scope of the project dictates what work is required to successfully achieve the project's objective. Discussions of project scope are focused on determining the specific boundaries of the project: what processes will be included and excluded, whether the project is going to result in a measurable operational improvement, if it needs to include audits or certification of the process, and so forth.

Defining the project scope should not be done in isolation; instead, you should gather input from multiple sources. These additional perspectives help ensure that you have a comprehensive overview, which in turn helps to prevent surprises and controversy later in the project. Some people to seek out in the early stages to provide advice and participate in your workshop include:

- Key users of the process who understand the details and can provide valuable input on the scope, required deliverables, and amount of work required. Their participation also aids in gaining their buy-in to the process changes, which is critical for deployment.

- Owners of closely related processes, who can provide requirements for your process's outputs.

- People who have done similar projects before and can provide many lessons learned and advice on how to run the project efficiently. Do not hesitate to invite people even if the projects they have run are only remotely similar.

- A facilitator who can lead the discussions, run the workshop, and keep it productive.

Begin the workshop by leading these participants to discuss the current situation and the desired to-be state. As the desired to-be state becomes clearer to the group, shift the focus to defining it. Discuss what part of the to-be state should be included in this project, and try to quantify what success in achieving it would look like. This can often be a difficult discussion, because of people's natural tendency to be all-inclusive and try to solve all of the world's problems, rather than limiting the scope to something manageable. Ultimately, the workshop group needs to define what is within the scope and out of the scope of the process improvement project. This can then be encapsulated into a sentence that can be used throughout the project as a communication tool to express the context within which project activities are chosen.

Conceptually, determining the scope of a project should be easy—you're simply identifying what will be worked on and what will not. However, like most theories, it's usually more difficult in practice since many perspectives need to be addressed, and individuals involved often don't agree. Each workshop is unique, and the facilitator needs to be prepared to actively manage the discussion. Attendees may express a wide range of reactions. Some groups dive into way too many details, while others have difficulty seeing beyond the most obvious in-scope items.

Once again, a whiteboard and sticky notes are handy tools for brainstorming. One approach to facilitating the scope of the discussion with a group of people is to draw a line on a whiteboard and write "In Scope" to the left of the line, and "Out of Scope" to the right. Ask all the team members to start listing individual scope items on sticky notes, focusing especially on items that border between being in and out of scope. Then have everyone put their sticky notes on the whiteboard on the appropriate side of the line, placing debatable items on the line itself.

As the input starts to slow down, get the group to focus on those debatable items. When it becomes difficult to gain agreement on a controversial topic, push toward creative definitions. You can change the definition of the topic or split it into two or more pieces with black-and-white divisions on what is in or out of scope. For instance, in the example earlier in this chapter with Bill, the manufacturing manager, it would make sense to say that only a part of the process system was in scope: setting up the hierarchy of a new section of procedures, while leaving the rest of the hierarchy and the process environment untouched. In your brainstorming session, there will usually be a few topics that could go either way and just need an arbitrary decision. Take care to ensure that the results of these decisions are clear to all who are involved in the discussions. These controversial topics can be specifically addressed in the statement defining the goal of the project, and they should be brought to the attention of your governance board for formal agreement/decision. Finding these items is one of the major goals of defining the project scope because the outcome of the associated discussion will define and shape your project. Remember, at this stage the results don't have to be perfect because the scope will continue to be refined going forward.

Defining the Project Goal

Once the team has a reasonably clear picture of what is in scope, try to formulate a concise sentence (twenty-five words is a good target) that embodies the object of this initiative. This sentence needs to clearly define what success looks like, in a way that's measurable and understandable by all those who will be involved in the project, and also include the desired timing. Here are some examples:

- Develop a system that allows the Customer Support team to access the latest maintenance procedures on their laptops at our customers' locations worldwide, and generate a feasibility report for the board of management meeting on November 15, 2014, based on a pilot implementation in Singapore.

- Reduce the manufacturing cycle time of product X3000 to five weeks by December 31, 2015, by streamlining and improving the usability of manufacturing procedures.

- Define and implement corrective actions identified for Purchasing in the September 2013 external audit, so that the 2014 audit results in no repeated findings related to Purchasing.

- Create a coherent business process system for the entire company, including the best practices and existing procedures from all divisions, and deploy it throughout the merged organization by September 30, 2016.

A number of techniques can be used to formulate these objective statements. One approach to facilitate the creation of the objective is to do some brainstorming after a thorough scope discussion has been held. Have each person write down her version of the objective statement with each word of the sentence on an individual sticky note. (Are you beginning to see why I find these so useful?) Then have everyone read their sentences and place the associated notes on the wall or table. After all have presented their versions, open the floor and let everyone take the individual words they like and start forming a new sentence in a collaborative way. Let the group create sticky notes with new words, move words around, and discuss what they're doing. The group typically comes to a quick conclusion on 75 percent of the sentence, then has more difficulty with the remaining portion.

During this process, the facilitator of the discussion should do the following:

- Ensure that the group agrees on the implications to the scope as the sentence evolves. Often during the discussion, the scope of the project can change, sometimes in significant ways, and these changes need to be understood by all.

- Guide the development of the sentence to make sure it includes an end target that's measurable. It must be entirely clear to all involved what success will look like when the initiative is done.

- Continually check that the sentence represents everything the participants want to achieve.

- As the sentence develops, try to extrapolate the type of activities that may be required to achieve the result, and make sure people agree that these types of activities are within the scope of the initiative.

At the conclusion of this section of the workshop, you should have:

- A clear project definition

- An agreed-upon vision of the to-be state

- A list of in-scope and out-of-scope items

- A list of controversial scope items that need formal agreement from the project board

- Project completion criteria

With this information, you can formulate a high-level project scope and project completion criteria that you can present to your governance board for approval.

DEFINING THE PROJECT EXECUTION STRATEGY

The second problem that frequently arises when executing process projects is that many of the actions outlined in this book required for successful process improvement need to be done in parallel. To make a process improvement "real," you need to address change management, which starts when the project starts and continues all the way through the completion of the project.

In this section, the word "strategy" is used to mean the basic approach taken to execute the process improvement within the defined scope of the project. The strategy ultimately dictates the activities needed to execute the project. Usually, several different approaches can be used to achieve the desired results. The difficulty is deciding which is the best strategy within the constraints. The optimal strategy for your project depends on its unique constraints. In this section, I give you some key points, specific to process improvement projects, that need to be addressed and included in the execution strategy.

Now that you have your project scope from the first day of the workshop, it's time to start thinking about what activities are required to realize the to-be state and to achieve the project goal. Below is a list of key areas you need to address when developing an execution strategy. You'll recognize most of them from previous chapters, but here we look at how they fit into the context of a project.

- *Division of work.* How do you plan to divide up the work? Will a few individuals do the work sequentially, or will many teams work in parallel? Is it better to break down the work based on your company's organization, by time phases, or by some other approach? Ultimately, these decisions determine the WBS for the project; as implied, the WBS can be set up in a number of different ways. Figure 14-1 shows a few common ways to organize a WBS—according to the life cycle of a project, the major deliverables created by a company, the structure of an organization, and the various locations of a global corporation. You want to select the WBS that best suits your company and your project.

- *Project controls.* What controls, governance structure, meetings, way of working, reporting, and Project Performance Indicators (PPIs) will you use to manage the project? How will you plan all the activities and track the progress? Will this simply be an action list tracked in a meeting, or will it be a detailed project plan? How will this information be analyzed to identify issues in time to solve them before they delay key deliverables? How will this information be consolidated into status reports for stakeholders?

- *Communication and stakeholder management.* Who are the key stakeholders and decision makers, how will you communicate to them, and at what frequency (communication plan)? What communication methods will you use during the rollout of the new process, as discussed in Chapter 10?

- *Process structure.* Do you need to develop a process structure or update an existing one? How will this procedure fit in with other existing ones? Are other related procedures being created, and how will these be kept in alignment?

- *Templates and tooling.* Are the templates and tools already in place, or does the project need to develop them? If they need to be developed or improved, how much of the process improvement work can be done before the updated tooling is in place?

- *Rollout strategy.* How will the procedure rollout be executed? Will the improvements be rolled out in one big bang, will there be a phased rollout, or will individual improvements be rolled out as they become available?

FIGURE 14-1   Options for Organizing a Work Breakdown
Structure

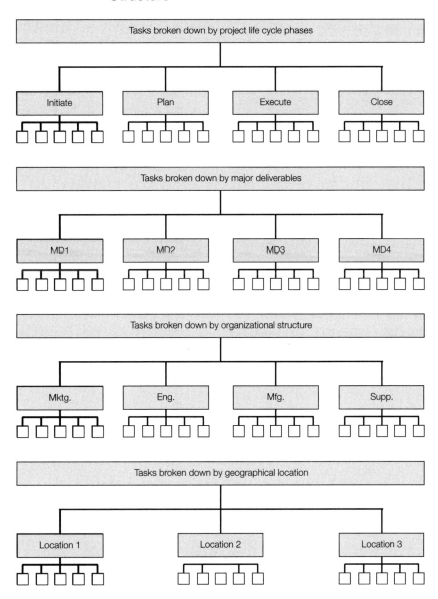

- *Testing.* Will the process be tested or piloted, and if so, how?

- *Training.* How will you train process users? How much training is required during the rollout, and how will the results of the training be confirmed? How will new users (e.g., new employees) be trained after the process is operational?

- *Confirmation and hand-over.* How do you confirm that you're done? Ideally, your project goal has a measurable target that can be used to clearly indicate when the initiative is done. If not, think through what is required to call this improvement initiative done and transition a process to normal operations. For example, do you need to pass an audit or verify that all the process KPIs are meeting target? Is there a control and monitoring plan in place, and who is responsible for executing it once the project is operational?

The intent of this list is to get you to think about the different aspects of a successful process improvement project. Your broad high-level strategy dictates how your project will tackle these different aspects within your unique constraints. This strategy becomes the foundation that you build the detailed schedule upon to ensure that the project team is working together. With this base, you can efficiently establish the time sequencing and interaction of each of the detailed activities such that the project is run efficiently.

CREATING A DETAILED PROJECT PLAN

Now that the strategy is in place and the high-level deliverables are known, the next step is to break the initiative down to more and more detailed levels of deliverables. This addresses the third problem discussed in the introduction to this chapter: not having enough details in the project to efficiently control the project. More important, it ensures that you have enough detail so that the team knows how to move forward in a unified manner. Breaking the activities down also allows you to proactively plan for iterations, thus avoiding the fourth problem with process improvement projects (as discussed below).

The ultimate goal should be to get the level of detail down to activities and deliverables that take five to ten working days to complete. These detailed deliverables can then be interlinked to a project schedule. At first, this may appear outrageously nitpicky, but striving for this level of detail has significant advantages:

- The process of breaking down the project to this level of detail provides direction and clarity, ensuring that your team truly understands what is required to complete the project successfully.

- The project leader will know within ten days if specific deliverables/activities are delayed. Too often, project leaders list one deliverable for a three-month task, such as "document Process X." Then the person writing this process consistently reports that everything is on track until Process X actually is supposed to be done. Only then does the project leader learn that minimal work has been done on the task, and the project is now delayed by three months.

- This level of detail provides information required to secure resources and justify the projected timeline. All too often, higher management thinks process improvement can be completed in ten person-hours or less. To combat this, you need clear and detailed information on what is truly required.

- These details can be used to form *Project Performance Indicators* to report status against. PPIs are much like KPIs, but they show the status of a *project* rather than a procedure. (A common PPI is percentage of project activities completed, which can be quantified in terms of the number of hours allotted for each activity.) In this way, your detailed schedule becomes the single "holy" source of data for status reports.

Typically, this level of detail is developed together with your team on the third day of the initial project workshop. Once you get started, it's usually not too difficult to continue to push the team to break down the work into the required level of detail. Choose a deliverable and ask what activities are required to produce it, and continue to break each one down into smaller parts until the resulting activities realistically take only five to ten days to complete and are defined clearly enough that their completion can be objectively verified.

All activities have been defined when you know how to produce all deliverables. The last steps are to interconnect the activities to show their relationships, and to assign owners. One method for doing this is to place every activity on a sticky note, place these notes on a large whiteboard or paper-covered wall, and start drawing connections with a marker. On the left-hand corner of each sticky note, add the duration of the activity; in the right-hand corner, add the owner. If your project is large, you may want to also add the amount of work in person-hours, not just the completion timing, to better estimate resource requirements. While the team is doing this, assign one person to start entering the data into your project plan software. At the completion of this activity, you have an initial draft of the project plan that identifies all activities needed to reach your goal, with owners and durations assigned. This data can then be reviewed and optimized to create your master project schedule. Now you can use the schedule to determine the duration of the whole project and estimate its resource requirements. In addition, you can use your project planning software (e.g., Microsoft Project) to simulate how different strategies affect the project timing and resource requirements.

Figure 14-2 is a sample project plan for developing one process in isolation. This project plan is generic enough to be used to create any process, if you make only minor adjustments associated with your specific project strategy. This project plan shows the desired level of detail and demonstrates how iterations can be included in the project plan. Information is provided in a table format, similar to project planning software formats, so that it can be easily displayed on these pages. Following the table are brief descriptions of each column in the table to help those unfamiliar with this format better understand the contents.

FIGURE 14-2 Sample Project Plan for a Project Improvement Initiative

ID	WBS	Task Name	Duration	Predecessors	Successors
1	1	Start improvement of Process X	0 days		3
2	2	- Create procedure	178 days		
3	2.1	Send meeting notice to core team	1 day	1	4,5
4	2.2	Prepare meeting agenda and secure facilitator	3 days	3	5
5	2.3	Delay until meeting happens	5 days	3,4	6
6	2.4	Meet with core team; create scope and goals and determine owner / team members	1 day	5	8,12,15,29
7	2.5	+ Create SIPOC	7 days		
11	2.6	- Create process map	83 days		
12	2.6.1	Send meeting notice to project team	1 day	6	13
13	2.6.2	Delay until meeting happens	5 days	12	14
14	2.6.3	Meet with process team to create and document process map	1 day	10,13	18
15	2.6.4	Obtain corporate document ID for the process document	1 day	6	16
16	2.6.5	Upload placeholder document into document management system	1 day	15	26
17	2.6.6	-Align process map with team, other processes, and stakeholders	22 days		
18	2.6.6.1	Find all linked processes	3 days	14	19
19	2.6.6.2	Document input/output discrepancies with linked processes	2 days	18	20,37
20	2.6.6.3	Update scope and process map	3 days	19	21,22
21	2.6.6.4	Set meeting of project team	1 day	20	24
22	2.6.6.5	Send to team for review	5 days	20	23
23	2.6.6.6	Update based on team feedback	2 days	22	25
24	2.6.6.7	Delay until meeting happens	5 days	21	25
25	2.6.6.8	Meet to review, revise, agree on process map	1 day	23,24	26
26	2.6.6.9	Send document for review by key stakeholders	5 days	16,25	27,41
27	2.6.6.10	Update process scope and map based on review	1 day	26	29,48,49
28	2.6.7	- Create procedure document	53 days		
29	2.6.7.1	Write initial draft	5 days	6,27	30
30	2.6.7.2	Send to team for review	5 days	29	31,32
31	2.6.7.3	Update based on team feedback	1 day	30	34

FIGURE 14-2 Continued

32	2.6.7.4	Set meeting of project team	1 day	30	33
33	2.6.7.5	Delay until meeting happens	5 days	32	34
34	2.6.7.6	Review and revise together, agree on procedure	1 day	31,33	35,48
35	2.6.7.7	Send to stakeholders for review	5 days	34	36
36	2.6.7.8	Update based on stakeholders' feedback	1 day	35	37,41,42,49
37	2.6.7.9	List process risks	2 days	19,36	38,41
38	2.6.7.10	Identify risk mitigation approaches	3 days	37	39
39	2.6.7.11	Document risk mitigation activities	1 day	38	40,49
40	2.6.7.12	Incorporate relevant risk mitigation activities in procedure	2 days	39	42
41	2.6.7.13	Identify and document KPIs that support process monitoring; include in procedure (optional)	5 days	26,36,37	42,52
42	2.6.7.14	Release document for review by project team, users, and other stakeholders	1 day	36,40,41	43
43	2.6.7.15	Project team, users, and other stakeholders provide input	10 days	42	44
44	2.6.7.16	Update process document based on review input	5 days	43	45
45	2.6.7.18	Upload draft document into document management system	1 day	44	57,64
46	2.7	+ Create rollout plan	17 days		
50	2.8	+ Create control and monitoring plan	15 days		
54	2.9	- Run real-world test and revise procedure	29 days		
55	2.9.1	+ Execute pilot	23 days		
60	2.9.2	- Update procedure based on results of pilot	6 days		
63	2.10	- Go live	64 days		
64	2.10.1	Deploy procedure company-wide	10 days	45,48,62	65
65	2.10.2	Initiate control and monitoring plan	0 days	53,64	66
66	2.10.3	Monitor process and provide startup support as required	40 days	65	67,68
67	2.10.4	Set up meeting with project governance board	1 day	66	69
68	2.10.5	Prepare material for decision to agree that process rollout is complete	10 days	66	69
69	2.10.6	Present process results to project governance board	1 day	67,68	70
70	2.10.7	Project governance board agrees process has been effectively deployed	0 days	69	71
71	2.10.8	Document and distribute meeting minutes	2 days	70	72
72	2.10.9	Celebrate success!!!	1 day	71	73
73	2.10.10	Process X improved and fully operational (End)	0 days	72	73

- *Column 1, ID:* This is a unique sequence identification that is used as a reference when linking activities.

- *Column 2, WBS:* This uses outline numbering to indicate an activity's place within the overall project work breakdown structure.

- *Column 3, Task Name:* This is a clear description of the activity or deliverable. It needs to be understandable by the people involved, and the completion of the activity must be verifiable.

- *Column 4, Duration:* This is how long (in business days) it realistically takes to complete the activity, not how much work it takes. For example, the duration of Task 35—"Send to stakeholders for review"—is five days even though the work required to review the document may be just a few hours. The extra days account for wait time until all stakeholders have gotten around to doing the review and providing feedback.

- *Column 5, Predecessors:* This contains the line numbers of all activities that must be completed before this activity can start. For example, Task 12—"Send meeting notice to project team"—cannot start until after the team members are determined in Task 6.

- *Column 6, Successors:* This contains the line numbers of all activities that depend on the completion of this activity, so it is the opposite of Predecessors. If Task 6 is a predecessor of Task 12, then Task 12 is a successor of Task 6.

Note: Most project management or spreadsheet software lets you open a higher-level task to see its component activities or close it for a higher-level view. Several tasks shown in Figure 14-2 with a plus symbol are closed (e.g., Task 2.7—"Create SIPOC"), hiding their lower-level activities.

All but one of the activities in Figure 14-2 achieve the goal of having a duration of ten days or less. Activity 66—"Monitor process and provide startup support as required"—breaks the rule since it extends for forty days. This is required to make sure that the process is functioning properly after it's deployed. Exceptions are allowed if you have a specific reason.

The schedule in Figure 14-2 provides an example of how to deal with the fact that process improvement is inherently iterative (the fourth problem, as discussed at the beginning of this chapter). Within the relatively simple activity of creating a process document, a number of iterations are embedded that build over time with increasing levels of detail. The first iteration starts with Task 17—"Align process map with team, other processes, and stakeholders." At this point, the only parts of the process that are defined are the goals, scope, and a rough process map. However, this step forces the project team to check all the inputs and outputs with other processes to confirm that everything is aligned. Then, in Task 20—"Update scope and process map"—specific time is allocated to update the document based on the findings of the review. Additional iterations include:

- *Tasks 21–23:* Team reviews the scope and initial draft of the process map.

- *Tasks 26–27:* Stakeholders review the process map.

- *Tasks 35–36:* Stakeholders review the first full draft of the procedure document.

- *Tasks 42–44:* Stakeholders and users review updated document after risks and KPIs are determined. (These could have been included in the initial document, but sometimes it's good to give people more time to become familiar with the process.)

- *Tasks 55–60:* Team reviews and updates the document based on results of a pilot implementation.

Embedding these iterations within the process creation, while also checking alignment with related processes, allows more to be done in parallel without the risk of significant rework. Ultimately, this maintains alignment and facilitates the efficient execution of a process improvement project.

Real-world sneaky tip: You may occasionally find it useful to link some activities in sequence even when they probably could be done in parallel. Artificially forcing the sequencing can help set clear steps and deadlines for the team. For instance, you can set up a separate task for writing each major section of a procedure, in place of the single Task 29 in Figure 14-2. What typically happens within a project is that after the first task's deadline is missed, you remind the task owner that he is late. Then he misses the second activity, and now you remind the task owner that he is late on two deliverables. At some point, the owner finally steps up and completes the entire block of work, often delivering the completed document ahead of schedule. This can be a huge benefit of creating a very detailed schedule.

Notice how the first problem, defining project completion criteria, was addressed in Figure 14-2. In this example, the "Document and Implement Process X" project is considered done when the following criteria are achieved:

- The process is updated and approved after a real-world pilot test and the signed document is uploaded into the corporate document management system (part of Task 60—"Update procedure based on results of pilot").

- The process has been fully deployed and is being used and monitored (Tasks 65–67).

- The project governance board agrees that the process has been effectively deployed (Task 70). Note that this is the only activity that specifically and directly addresses the quality of the process and its deployment. Ideally, quality aspects of the process should be added throughout the plan. In this example, an additional quality criteria could have been added by adding an activity such as "Verify that the desired KPI performance metric has been achieved for three consecutive months." If this were added, you would also need additional activities to iteratively achieve this target.

In some cases, a single project or program may involve revising or creating more than one process. In that case, the tasks listed in Figure 14-2 are still applicable, but they would be only a subset of all project activities. You'd need to repeat all activities for *each* process you're revising, and you would need some additional iterations and reviews to make sure that all your processes aligned with each other.

At the conclusion of the project workshop, you have a very detailed project plan that breaks down the work into clear measurable pieces that have buy-in from the people involved. The plan shows the interrelationship between the activities. This detailed plan becomes the reference to measure your project against. Ideally, you won't need to update this plan, but that's not realistic. It is very difficult to identify all required activities in advance, so over the life of the project, you'll probably need to update the plan to reflect the latest learning. Adding a project plan review into your schedule at a specific frequency, such as once every three months, can be a good idea. For very long projects, another way to work is to develop a detailed project plan for only the next three months, leaving activities further out undetailed. Then, at your regular plan reviews, you can flesh out the details for the next three months and add them to the plan. (This is called "rolling-wave planning.")

EXECUTING THE PROJECT

Now that the project is defined, the strategy is clear, and the detailed project plan is in place, all that's left is execution. Executing a process system improvement project is not significantly different from executing any other project, but it does require special attention from the project leader on coaching and messaging.

Coaching is often required in process improvement projects, since the required information needs to be pulled from a broad range of employees and managers at different levels of the organization. Often, these people are not process experts. They may not understand the overall picture of what you are trying to achieve, and they don't know how to do some of the things you are asking them to do. Be prepared to provide these people with the help and assistance they need to properly support the project.

Every communication and action you perform as the project leader sends a message. You need to control your message and keep it on target at all times to drive the change you want. This is critical for these types of projects because uncontrolled messages can end up engendering resistance to change that wouldn't happen otherwise.

By spending a little extra time up front clearly defining the project, developing a strategy, creating a project plan, and putting some extra attention in areas that are critical for process improvement projects, you are setting a foundation for successful process improvement.

AFTERWORD

WHEN IT COMES TO process improvements, there's never only one right way to do it—just some basic principles. For any process improvement initiative, there may be a hundred ways to do it right and a thousand ways to do it wrong. What I've tried to do in this book is explain those principles and show the basic tasks and flow in setting up a process system and realizing your procedures. I've also provided specific examples of ways to manage your processes that have worked well in practice. Armed with these, you're ready to make an informed decision about what will work for your business, given your environment's specific constraints and culture.

REMEMBERING THE UNDERLYING PRINCIPLES

In the Introduction to this book, I stated three basic principles:

1. Processes work best when they are part of a managed and coherent system.

2. To make a documented process useful, you need to launch it successfully and then monitor, measure, and improve it on an ongoing basis.

3. There is no one right way to build a process or process system. To have one that works for your business, you need to customize it.

I'm adding one more principle to that list: No process is important in itself—it's what it does for your business that matters. It's easy to get wrapped up in process improvement for its own sake. Avoid this by keeping your business goals and customer needs in view, and design your procedures to satisfy those.

UNDERSTANDING THAT
NO PROCESS IS AN ISLAND

Here's a quick way to avoid success in business: Set up every department as an independently functioning entity, and discourage communication among departments. The process structure can be seen as the network uniting all parts of your business. It defines how each procedure is connected to the next in line, ensuring that there are no gaps so that each one gets the inputs it needs and in turn produces the outputs required.

The other part of the process system is the process environment, which defines a standard way to create and maintain your procedures, to deliver them to their users, and to manage their operation. This ensures that process creators work efficiently and don't forget important steps (like consulting process users!). When procedures use a standard format and are stored in a single repository, users know where to find the procedures they need and where to find the information they want inside procedures.

Strive to keep both the structure and the environment as simple and intuitive as they can be. Remember that your customer for both is not the quality department but the process stakeholders: process owners, procedure users, managers who need to monitor these procedures to see how well their business operates, and the customers for process outputs (including, ultimately, your end customers). If the process system isn't working well for them, then it's not good enough. When creating or revising a process system, remember your stakeholders. Whenever there's a question about how to design any aspect of a process system or procedure, try to choose the option that's best for their needs.

MAKING YOUR PROCEDURES MORE THAN PAPER

Creating a good procedure requires considering multiple needs, and then revising through several iterations until everyone is in agreement. Start by defining the scope and goals of your procedure, then work from the outside in. Determine the inputs and outputs first, with the suppliers/customers for each one, and then map the tasks within the procedure. Finally, create a complete document with detailed information to support the process map. Consult your stakeholders at each stage, and revise to incorporate their feedback.

That's not enough, though, to ensure a successful working procedure. Don't wait until you're done documenting to begin planning the implementation of your procedure. Once you have enough basic information and have a good handle on who will be involved in the procedure, what they need to know, and what infrastructure is required to support them, begin creating your rollout plan and your control and monitoring plan.

Remember that you'll need to go through all of this again the next time you create or improve a procedure. Once you've executed your plans and your procedure is running, call the team back together and figure out what lessons you can learn. What went well? What didn't go so well? How can you do better next time? Write these lessons down and (this is the hard part!) consult them before you go to work on your next process improvement initiative. Share them so others can learn from you, and ask other teams to share their own lessons with you.

FACILITATING CONVERSATIONS, DRIVING CHANGE, AND MANAGING YOUR PROJECTS

Part 5 of this book discusses skills you need to succeed in making improvements and in making them stick. None of these are particularly easy, but experience helps. Practice. Experiment. See what works for you. There are books, classes, and websites devoted to each of these topics. Each topic is complex, and I've only scratched the surface here and provided a few takeaway points:

- Whenever you're having a meeting or workshop in which you need to gather input from all participants, an independent facilitator can be invaluable. A facilitator's job is to keep the conversation on target, make sure everyone is heard, and guide the participants to alignment.

- If you're trying to drive change in an organization, consider two channels: top-down through the management hierarchy, and bottom-up through getting buy-in at the grassroots level. Tailor your message to your audience's concerns, and try to adapt the environment to make the new way of working easy and intuitive.

- Most process improvement initiatives are run as projects. If you take time up front to organize your team and develop a detailed project plan, you greatly increase your chances of finishing successfully—on time and on budget with targets achieved.

* * *

Within this book is a lot of information on how to follow these principles to build a useful process system, and to work within it to create, launch, and operate standard procedures. I've included examples and recommendations based on what has worked for me and others, and I hope you will find them helpful. Bear in mind, though, that outside the covers of this book you can find much more information and many more discussions on process systems and how to implement processes. New ideas, tools, and methodologies are released every year, each claiming to help you build procedures to make your business better. Now you have the ability to choose, design, or adapt your own methods, decide on tooling, and create a system of procedures that will help your company do business effectively and improve continually. Success!

Sample Procedure Template

Company Name LOGO	
Procedure [Title goes here]	
Summary [Short summary of procedure and its purpose here]	
Author [Author name here]	**Date of Last Revision** [Date here]
Process Owner [Name and role here]	
Company Confidential	

(Continued on next page)

Table of Contents
Insert table of contents for this document here.

Introduction

Goals
Describe the goals of the process here (e.g., "This procedure provides the standard method for performing annual employee reviews at XYZ company.").

Scope
Describe the scope of the process here (e.g., what are process boundaries—where does it begin, where does it end, what is and is not included? What is the process trigger—that is, how do you know when this process needs to be executed?). Optional: List parent procedure, child procedures, and interlocking procedures on same level.

Process Map
Insert a process map here. Sample:

RACI

Insert table explaining who is Responsible (R), Accountable (A), Contributing (C), or Informed (I) regarding each step in the process.

Step #	Name of process step	Role 1 (e.g., Engineer)	Role 2 (e.g., Manager)	Role 3 (e.g., HR rep)
1	[Step name here]	R	A	I
2	[Step name here]	C	R	A
3	[Step name here]	R	A	C
4	[Step name here]	I	R	A
5	[Step name here]	I	I	R

Additional Details

Include anything here that isn't obvious from looking at the process map (e.g., further description of each task).

KPIs

Include the KPIs here (e.g., how will this process be measured?).

Definitions and Acronyms

Define any unusual terms or unusual uses of common terms, and spell out any acronyms.

List of References

Insert any documents users might need to check for more information (e.g., governing documents, standards, related procedures).

(Continued on next page)

Records

Make note of any records produced as a result of this process and kept for future reference or as proof of the execution of the process.

	Name	Document number (if applicable)	Location	Retention period
1				
2				
3				

INDEX

accountability
  for process, 40
  in RACI matrix, 127
  for resources, 217
achievable target value for KPIs, 185
actions, based on KPIs, 191–192
activities
  duration of, 235–236
  in sequence vs. in parallel, 237
activity-based approach, to process
    management, 40
administrative work, for procedures, 214
agenda for meeting, 200–201
analysis paralysis, 109
approval of procedures, 44, 57
  governance structure and, 222
  individuals involved, 103
AS9100, 40
audience, training materials for
    international, 175
audits
  avoiding traps, 151
  for certification, 17
  internal, 176
  unused procedures and, 19–20
authority, 41
  delegating, 79

best practices, 110
big picture, responsibility for
    understanding, 78–79
Black Box approach, 113–120
bottom line, management support and,
    208–209
bottom-up change, 207, 210–212, 244
  disadvantage of, 208
  vs. top-down, 78

BPMN (Business Process Modeling
    Notation), 66
brainstorming, 64
  example, 130–131
  facilitator for, 198
  leading session, 203–204
  sticky notes for process flow, 124
  whiteboard for, 224
branches, in process maps, 140
business analysis, 3
business case
  components of, 100
  estimating costs and savings, 209–210
Business Process Modeling Notation
    (BPMN), 66
buy-in from management, obtaining,
    70–71

calculation methods, for KPIs, 189
Capability Maturity Model Integration
    (CMMI), 59–61
Carnegie Mellon University, Software
    Engineering Institute (SEI), 59
certification audits, 17
champion, for process, 102
changes
  bottom-up vs. top-down channel
      for, 78
  communicating, 166–173
  person requesting, 99
  planning, 91–111
  in procedure interrelationships, 51
  reasons for, 211
  resistance to, 213–216
  strategies to implement, 207–208
  types, 94–95
child procedure, 47

249

ABOUT THE AUTHOR

PAULA K. BERMAN has acquired her knowledge of process systems and process improvement from her experience at companies ranging from under a hundred to over a hundred-thousand employees in several different industries. She holds a Bachelor's degree in Mechanical Engineering and a Master's degree in Physical Sciences, and qualified as a Six Sigma Black Belt while working at Honeywell Aerospace. While working for ASML, a leader in semiconductor capital equipment, Paula had the opportunity to live and work in Europe and Asia, adding to the breadth of her background. Her varied experience has helped her develop a holistic approach to business process implementation and practical solutions for getting results.

Outside work, Paula reads whenever possible, including during her other hobbies of knitting and traveling. Occasionally she puts the book down to go rowing. She lives in Hillsboro, Oregon, with her husband and two cats.